NOT FOREVER ON EARTH

NOT FOREVER

PREHISTORY OF MEXICO

ON EARTH

By Shirley Gorenstein

Photographs by Lee Boltin

CHARLES SCRIBNER'S SONS · NEW YORK

Text copyright © 1975 Shirley Gorenstein

Photographs copyright © 1975 Lee Boltin

Library of Congress Cataloging in Publication Data

Gorenstein, Shirley.
    Not forever on earth.

    1. Indians of Mexico—Antiquities. 2. Mexico—
History. 3. Indians of Central America—Antiquities.
4. Central America—Antiquities. I. Title.
F1219.G67   970.4′2   73–1366
ISBN 0–684–13837–9

1 3 5 7 9 11 13 15 17 19   V/C   20 18 16 14 12 10 8 6 4 2

PRINTED IN THE UNITED STATES OF AMERICA

Title-page illustration: Mural from Teotihuacan, partially restored. The motifs are religious; the graceful animals are mythical. The colors were originally brilliant hues of blue, dark red, pink, yellow, and green on a white background.

TO CAROLL

Truly do we live on earth?
Not forever on earth; only a little while here.
Although it be jade, it will be broken,
Although it be gold, it is crushed,
Although it be quetzal feather, it is torn asunder.
Not forever on earth; only a little while here.

Attributed to King Nezahuacóyotl
(Hungry Coyote) of Texcoco, 1402–1472

CONTENTS

ILLUSTRATIONS

ILLUSTRATIONS

MAPS

PREFACE

The primary responsibility of archaeologists is to reconstruct the history and culture of prehistoric times, and they have succeeded in producing a narrative for most of the world through millions of years of archaeologically recorded time. Yet archaeologists also have the opportunity of exploring a phenomenon just out of the reach of the historian and the cultural anthropologist: the trajectory of profound societal change. Only the archaeologist has available the information which shows the metamorphosis of a simple hunting and gathering life to a complex urban society. In Mexico a dynamic force which runs throughout the area's prehistory expresses the transformation that took place there. In this book I try to show what archaeologists have learned about the unique culture history of pre-Hispanic Mexico and the development of its complex society.

I first understood the need for synthesis in archaeology in long tutorial conversations with William Duncan

Strong. I cling to the remembered shreds of his remarks, for they continue to be a rich resource for guiding my own attempts at finding patterns. To Gordon F. Ekholm I am indebted for the gift of appreciating Mexican archaeology. More recently I have learned much about the interpretation of cultural change from Edward P. Lanning. I owe to John Hyslop, historian turned anthropologist, a better understanding of the differences between historical and anthropological perspectives in viewing events through time.

I have always been grateful for the opportunity to work in Mexico. While this privilege was extended through the generosity of my Mexican colleagues, I would not have fared half so well were it not for the endless kindness and support of two Mexican families, the Davidoffs and the Sonís. Their efforts on my behalf can be compared only to those I have known within my own family. I hope that through my work I can give them in exchange some further knowledge of the prehistory of their country.

Finally I am indebted to John Cole for his research assistance. His knowledge of the history of anthropology has been invaluable to me. I thank Ethan Ezra Gorenstein for his meticulous reading of the first draft and Gabriel William Gorenstein for his attention to the compilation of the bibliography.

NOT FOREVER ON EARTH

1

EXPLORERS INTO THE PAST

CIVILIZATION, represented by a high level of social organization and a large, dense population differentiated according to wealth, occupation, and control of power, arose indigenously in only two places in the New World: Mexico and Peru. Both areas were overrun and their cultures destroyed by the Spaniards in the sixteenth century, but from the conquests Europeans learned of the complexity and richness of the native societies. They found it hard to believe that states and empires, palaces and pyramids, sculpture and painting, and a thousand other elaborations of human existence had occurred so far from European culture.

In the hundred years or so after the Spanish conquests,

3

conquerors, priests, and civil administrators described the life they found. Since it took a considerable time for the Spaniards to undermine native society, many of the descriptions contain excellent accounts of what life was like before they came.

By the seventeenth century the great tradition of native culture in Mexico was gone. It had joined the past that could be known only through writings and ruins. In the next two hundred years explorers and travelers visited the ruins with the same attitude as that with which their contemporaries were making expeditions to classical Greek, Roman, and Egyptian ruins: they wanted to discover the past. These men were not archaeologists, but antiquaries; they were not concerned with the native Indian history or lifeways, but only with the beauty of the ruins and the artifacts found among them. Some of their accounts of the ruins were published in Viscount Kingsborough's nine-volume work, *Antiquities of Mexico*, which appeared between 1831 and 1848. The descriptions were brief but useful and in most cases were the first orderly accounts of archaeological sites.

The most important American traveler in Mexico during the nineteenth century was John Lloyd Stephens, who, with Frederick Catherwood, an English draftsman, visited the Mayan ruins in Yucatán, Guatemala, and Honduras. Stephens's books, *Incidents of Travel in Central America, Chiapas, and Yucatan* (1841) and *Incidents of Travel in Yucatan* (2 vols., 1843) were concerned primarily with the perils of travel and the native customs and only secondarily with detailed descriptions of the ruins. Nevertheless, his accounts of what the ruins looked like in the nineteenth century are invaluable for present reconstruction, and Catherwood's drawings provide details

4

of architecture which photographic techniques could not duplicate for more than a hundred years.

By the end of the nineteenth century archaeology was emerging as a branch of learning concerned with the systematic recovery and study of material evidence of the past. The transformation of antiquarianism into archaeology came about because the educated men who were then visiting ruins had shifted their focus from adventures of exploration and observation of the picturesque to concern with the historical importance of the ruins themselves. Descriptions became more detailed, and drawings of architecture and artifacts exhaustive rather than partial.

Two important bodies of work of this kind were published around the turn of the century. The first was William H. Holmes's *Archaeological Studies among the Ancient Cities of Mexico* (1895–1897). It contained architectural studies of major ruins that could be mapped without excavation. The drawings of the sites were done with a "panoramic view," and this orientation gave simultaneously not only the plans of the buildings, but also details of structures. The subtitles of the introduction offer an idea of Holmes's range of interests: monumental remains; function of buildings; the architect and his plan; instruments of precision; orientation and assemblage; building materials; transportation (of such materials); stone cutting and sculpture; masonry stucco work and painting; substructures; stairways; superstructures; wall surfaces; ceilings; roofs; doorways and other wall openings; columns and pillars; and, finally, hieroglyphs.

The second major work was the five volumes of *Biologia Centrali-Americana* (1889–1902) by Alfred Percival Maudslay, a member of the British colonial service. He produced photographs, maps, and plans of the ruins in

5

southern Mexico, Guatemala, and Honduras, along with drawings of the ruins by Miss Annie Hunter and photographs of the hieroglyphs.

About this time, the hieroglyphs began to receive special attention, mainly from two men, Ernst W. Förstemann and J. Thompson Goodman. Förstemann, a German, and head librarian of the Dresden Royal Public Library, was fifty-eight years old when he turned to this investigation, and he continued with it without interruption and with great energy until his death in 1906 at the age of eighty-four. Goodman, an American journalist, owned and edited *The Territorial Enterprise,* published in Virginia City, Nevada, and in 1862 hired Mark Twain to serve on its staff. If Mark Twain knew of his employer's exotic interest, no whisper appears in his writing. Certainly there seem no worlds farther apart than those of the rural United States and temple Maya. There is some question as to whether Goodman, who published slightly later, was aware of Förstemann's work. While Goodman made no public acknowledgment of Förstemann's contributions, he, like Förstemann, solved numerous problems concerning the mathematics and calendrical system of the ancient peoples of Mexico.

But the greatest contributor to the study of pre-Hispanic Mexico was Eduard Seler, another German, who had been appointed to reorganize the national museum of Mexico. During the years 1902–1923 he published his great five-volume work entitled *Gesammelte Abhandlungen zur Amerikanischen Sprach und Altertumskunde (Collected Essays on American Language and Archaeology).* It is an extraordinary achievement of interpretation and synthesis, using all sources of data: the pictorial documents of the native Mexicans (the codices), the Spanish chronicles, and the existing archaeology.

The archaeology of Mexico took a new turn in the first decades of the twentieth century. The archaeological sites that were known by the end of the nineteenth century were those which had not needed excavation. Since they had never been completely covered by the soil and the jungle growth, they had remained, at least in part, visible to the explorer. A considerable number had been recorded by one writer or another. Finding sites and describing them, however, was only the first step. The next goal was to place them in some historical sequence. In other words, the major work of the early twentieth century was to give time depth to the prehistory of Mexico. Professional archaeologists, trained with theories and methods for conducting this kind of investigation, began to work on the problem of chronology in central Mexico.

Three great sites were known there: Tenochtitlán, where Mexico City now stands, Tula, some 100 kilometers to the north in the state of Hidalgo, and Teotihuacan, in the Valley of Mexico, about 50 kilometers north of Mexico City.

American archaeologists, probably influenced by the practice of their better-known counterparts who were studying classical Greece, Rome, and the Near East, turned to the documentary evidence to provide a scaffolding. The Spanish documents gave clear and specific information about the people living in Mexico at the time of the conquest. There was no doubt that Tenochtitlán was the Aztec capital, but the native pictorial documents and legends which recorded history before this time were fragmentary and filled with confusing references. They seemed to say that the people before the Aztecs were the Toltecs, and therefore Tula and Teotihuacan were presumed to be Toltec centers. In fact, all sites in central Mexico with spectacular architecture that were not Aztec were considered Toltec.

The void before so-called Toltec was an inviting but unknown time. One way of reaching it, since the documentary records went back only to Toltec, was through excavation and the principle of superposition. This principle, noted by geologists in the middle of the nineteenth century and adopted by archaeologists, is simple. The layers of the earth are set down through time, therefore the older layers lie below the younger ones. With this guide archaeologists could enter that predocumentary chasm.

Manuel Gamio, a Mexican archaeologist with training at Columbia University, dug at the site of Azcapatzalco in 1909 and found, in layers from top to bottom, Aztec, then Toltec, and below those, material which he named "Hill Culture." In the next decade the Hill Culture was the focus of attention. Zelia Nuttall, a highly educated North American though not quite a professional archaeologist, had purchased some Hill Culture figurines in the vicinity of the Pedregal, the area of lava flow just outside the heart of Mexico City. Gamio decided that there must be a Hill Culture occupation under the lava flow. He tunneled under the lava and was rewarded by the find of an ancient graveyard, called Copilco, which was rich in artifacts lying in association with the skeletal remains.

Gamio became even more intensely interested in time depth but in a more sophisticated way. Now he was concerned not only with how far back in time Mexican cultures went, but also in the continuity and development of culture. Since he could not begin at the beginning and work his way upward, he chose to follow archaeological field techniques by working from what was known, the top layers, to what was unknown, the lower layers. He selected the subvalley of Teotihuacan in the larger Valley of Mexico as the site of his investigation. He traced the culture history of that smaller valley from contemporary back to prehistoric times, using both ethnographic and archaeological sources. The result, published in three volumes in 1922, was called *La Población del Valle de Teotihuacán (The Population of the Valley of Teotihuacán)*. It earned him a Ph.D. at Columbia University and was an enormous contribution to the understanding of Mexican prehistory. Not only was it a detailed and comprehensive study of the cultures as they were known up to that time; it also established the principles that these cultures must be looked at sequentially and continuity and development examined in detail.

Archaeologists were also becoming concerned with two other aspects of Mexican prehistory: the origin of Mexican culture and the interrelationship through time of cultures in different parts of Mexico. Herbert Spinden, a curator at the Brooklyn Museum in New York City, re-evaluated the available data and provided some ways of thinking about these problems. He renamed the Hill Culture the "Archaic Horizon" and designated it as coming after the culture of the first migrants to the New World from Asia. Spinden saw in the character of the Archaic Horizon in the Valley of Mexico—lacking as it did a developed religion and symbolic art—the hearth of all later Mexican culture. It was there, he wrote, that agriculture, pottery making, and loom weaving were invented, and it was from there that these technologies spread to the rest of Mexico—and indeed to South America, where culture developed in slightly different ways.

9

The idea of the Archaic Horizon became very important to North American archaeologists working in Mexico. One of them, George C. Vaillant, had studied at Harvard and done field work in the southwestern United States and southern Mexico. In 1927 he was made a curator of Mexican archaeology at the American Museum of Natural History in New York and there began to work closely with Clarence Hay, a trustee of the museum and an associate of Gamio. Hay suggested to Vaillant that the most interesting problem in Mexican archaeology was the clarification of the Archaic Horizon. To this end Vaillant began a series of investigations in and around the Valley of Mexico. Using pottery and figurines that he found in the layers of the earth, he established a series of cultural changes that he postulated had occurred within the time span of the Archaic Horizon. He also noticed that the materials he was finding in the bottom layers (the early Archaic Horizon) were not simple; indeed they represented a fairly complex culture, which, he reasoned, could not have developed from the lifeways of the Asian nomads. There must be a culture or cultures between that of the Asian nomads and the Archaic Horizon. And the Archaic Horizon was between that early culture and the Toltecs and Aztecs. In other words, instead of the Archaic Horizon's being near the beginning, it was somewhere in the middle, and Vaillant changed its name to the "Middle Cultures."

Having clarified the chronological position of the Archaic Horizon, Vaillant next turned to the investigation of the cultural content of the Middle Cultures, in which he was joined by Samuel Lothrop, an archaeologist affiliated with the Heye Foundation, who had worked on the Middle Cultures of Central America. Together the two men

10

identified a group of traits which occurred mostly in Central America and did not occur in the Middle Cultures of the Valley of Mexico. They termed these traits the "Q-complex" and suggested that they had originated in South America and moved through Central America north to Mexico. The controversy concerning the independent development and diffusion of the high cultures in Mexico and Peru was thus clearly set forth, with Spinden on one side and Vaillant and Lothrop on the other.

Another outcome of Vaillant's close and careful examination of the content of the Middle Cultures was the recognition that there were differences in the development of culture in the various parts of Mexico and that different archaeological regions within Mexico needed to be defined and described.

In the 1930s a great deal of work was done in this direction, sponsored by the Carnegie Institution of Washington under the supervision of Alfred Kidder of Harvard University, who was appointed chairman of the Institution's Division of Historical Research in 1929. Field work was conducted primarily in southern Mexico, Guatemala, and Honduras. Within this area regions were defined, described, and related to one another as well as to the better-known sequence in the Valley of Mexico.

At the same time Mexican archaeologists such as Alfonso Caso and Eduardo Noguera were working at important sites in central Mexico outside of the Valley of Mexico. Other archaeologists, both Mexican and North American, were locating sites in northern, eastern, and western Mexico and describing the regional sequences. By the 1940s the various archaeological regions of Mexico had been defined and the broad outlines of pre-Hispanic Mexico's culture history were beginning to be drawn.

In the 1940s a discovery took place which upset the previous accepted chronology for the Valley of Mexico to which many of the other regional chronologies were tied. The discovery was sparked by a Mexican historian, Wigberto Jiménez Moreno, who identified Toltec place names in the documentary sources with sites in the vicinity of Tula. This led him to postulate that Tula was the Toltec capital and that Teotihuacan was not Toltec at all. Working with this hypothesis, Jorge Acosta, a leading Mexican archaeologist, began excavations at Tula. At the bottom layers he found post-Teotihuacan pottery. It was clear, then, that Teotihuacan was not contemporary with Tula but earlier. Not only were the Toltecs not at Teotihuacan, they did not come to Tula until after the destruction of Teotihuacan. The sequence for the Valley of Mexico now became: Nomads, Early Cultures, Middle Cultures, Teotihuacan, the Toltecs at Tula, and finally the Aztecs at Tenochtitlán.

Archaeologists had now learned enough about sequence in various Mexican regions—not just in the Valley of Mexico—to look for a general chronological framework for the whole area, into which they could fit the regional sequences. In order to do this they had to find out what "the whole area" was. Having located the individual trees they now had to find the forest. It would have been simple if the area of pre-Hispanic high culture had been congruent with the present political boundaries of Mexico. But most of northern Mexico did not have the complex cultural remains of central and southern Mexico. And the early nineteenth-century explorers had found complex pre-Hispanic cultures in Guatemala, Honduras, and British Honduras. Was there any cultural gap between Mexico and the southernmost region of the Andes of South

America? Both Spinden with his notion of the Archaic Horizon and Vaillant and Lothrop with their idea of the "Q-complex" had focused on spatial continuity.

In 1943 the Mexican ethnologist Paul Kirchhoff offered a solution to the problem of the relation of Mexico to Central and South America in pre-Hispanic times which has been accepted, with some subsequent modifications, by all archaeologists. In an article entitled "Mesoamerica" he analyzed the distribution of the cultural traits and languages in existence at the time of the conquest from the southern United States into Mexico and Central America and down into the Andean and Amazon regions of South America. By comparing the distributions as he was able to isolate the area that he called Mesoamerica. The northern boundary began at the Río Fuerte in Sinaloa in western Mexico, dipped deep into central Mexico, and rose in the east to the Río Panuco in Veracruz. The southern boundary ran southeast from the mouth of the Motagua River in the Gulf of Honduras through Lake Nicaragua to the Gulf of Nicoya on the west coast of Costa Rica.

The traits which Kirchhoff considered as defining the Mesoamerican area were:

A certain type of digging stick (coa); the construction of gardens by reclaiming land from lakes (chinampas); the cultivation of lime-leaved sage (chía) and its use for a beverage and for oil to give luster to paints; the cultivation of the century plant (maguey) for its juice (aguamiel), fiber for clothing and paper, and maguey beer (pulque); the cultivation of cacao; the grinding of corn softened with ashes or lime.

Clay bullets for blow-guns, lip plugs and other trinkets of clay; the polishing of obsidian; pyrite mirrors;

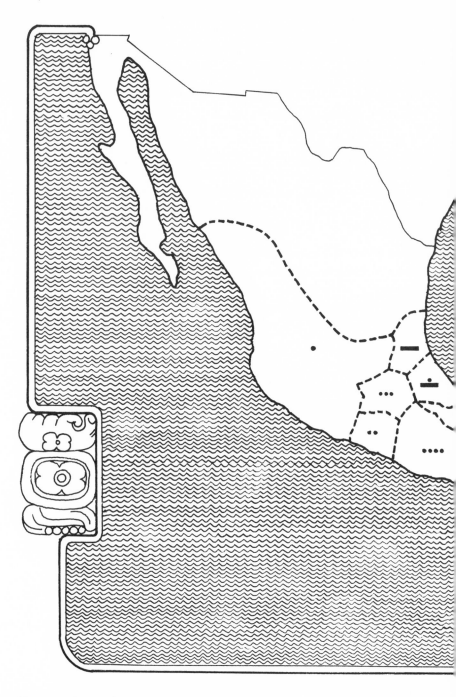

Mesoamerican culture areas

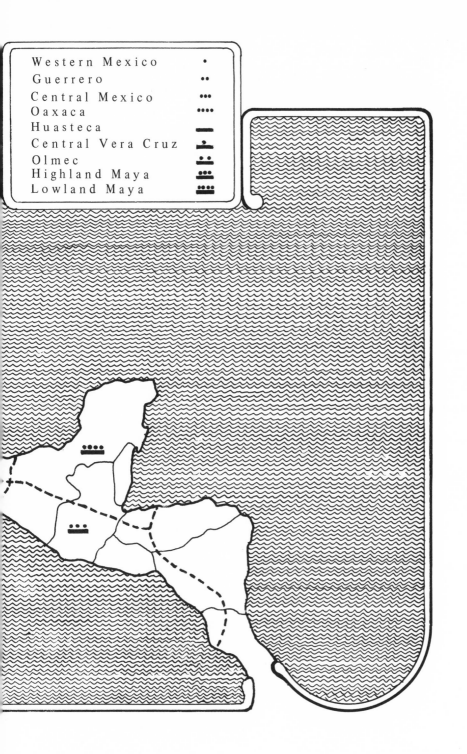

Western Mexico	•
Guerrero	••
Central Mexico	•••
Oaxaca	••••
Huasteca	▬
Central Vera Cruz	▬••
Olmec	▬••
Highland Maya	▬•••
Lowland Maya	▬••••

copper tubes to drill stones; the use of rabbit hair to adorn textiles; wooden swords with flint or obsidian chips along the edges (*macuahuitl*); corselets padded with cotton (*ichcahuipilli*); shields with two hand-grips. Turbans; sandals with heels; one-piece suits for warriors. Step pyramids, stucco floors, ball courts with rings. Hieroglyphic writing; signs for numerals and relative value of these according to position; books folded screen-style; historical annals and maps.

Year of 18 months of 20 days, plus 5 additional days; combination of 20 signs and 13 numerals to form a period of 260 days; combination of the two previous periods to form a cycle of 52 years; festivals at the end of certain periods; good and bad omen days; persons named according to the days of their birth.

Ritual use of paper and rubber; sacrifices of quail; certain forms of human sacrifice (burning people alive; dancing dressed in the skin of the victim); certain forms of self-sacrifice (extraction of one's blood from the tongue, ears, legs, sexual organs); the flying game or ritual (*juego del volador*); 13 as a ritual number; a series of divinities; . . . concept of several other worlds and of a difficult journey to them; drinking the water in which the deceased relative has been bathed.

Specialized markets or markets subdivided according to specialties; merchants who are at the same time spies; military orders (eagle knights and tiger knights); wars for the purpose of securing sacrificial victims. (Kirchhoff, "Mesoamerica," in Sol Tax, ed., *Heritage of Conquest*, 1952, pp. 24–25.)

By isolating Mesoamerica, Kirchhoff laid the ground-work for also defining the boundaries of a western South America culture area and of the Intermediate Area between the two. Archaeologists are still trying to discover how civilizations arose independently in Mesoamerica and western South America, while recognizing that many traits must have diffused by land and water from one civilization to the other.

The definition of Mesoamerica helped archaeologists to break time into historically meaningful periods. The Mesoamerican traits listed by Kirchhoff showed the end of a historical development. The archaeological record indicated that this distinctive tradition began to emerge around 1500 B.C. That date was considered to mark the commencement of the Preclassic period. The end of the Preclassic was dated A.D. 250. From then until about A.D. 900 was the period called the Classic. Between 900 and the conquest in 1519—the period called the Postclassic—important developments occurred in the military and political systems. Currently this division of periods is being questioned as not sufficiently precise and not equally appropriate in all regions.

The time before the advent of the Mesoamerican tradition has been divided into two periods. The first is called the Paleo-Indian or Paleo-American and refers to the time when the nomads whose ancestors came from Asia entered the Mesoamerican area and supported themselves primarily by hunting. This subsistence pattern lasted until about 7000 B.C. Then there was an increase in wild-plant collecting, which preceded the beginning of plant cultivation. The second period, from 7000 to 1500 B.C., is characterized by experiments with cultivation but continued reliance on wild-plant collecting and on hunting and has been called, rather awkwardly, Food-Collecting and Incipient Cultivation.

In the mid-twentieth century archaeological thinking in North America again changed its focus. This came about largely as a result of a monograph by the American anthropologist Walter Taylor, entitled A *Study of Archaeology* and published by the American Anthropological Association in 1948. Taylor attacked American archaeologists in general, but his main assault was against Alfred Kidder and the work of the Carnegie Institution in Mexico, Honduras, and Guatemala. His thesis was that archaeologists should not be historians of culture, concentrating on specific events, times, and places, but anthropologists, investigating the nature of culture, the ways it develops, and how and why it becomes more complicated. The whole subsequent trend of archaeology has been affected by his admonitions. Culture history was not abandoned but it became more interpretive, and for the first time the writings of archaeologists were concerned primarily with the reasons for cultural change and the processes by which it comes about.

2

LEGACY FROM PREHISTORIC TIMES

ARCHAEOLOGY has sometimes been defined as the study of cultural behavior from material remains. While other branches of knowledge are also concerned with cultural behavior, only archaeologists use material remains as their sole source of data. They are concerned with all material remains that have survived and particularly with things manufactured by man, such as settlements, architecture, ceramic vessels, stone tools, gold and silver jewelry. While archaeologists are also interested in remains not manufactured by man but used by him, such as the berries he gathered, the plants he cultivated, and the ani-

19

mals he killed, the manufactured things, which are called artifacts, have received their closest attention.

Perhaps the most important piece of information the archaeologist needs for understanding the men of the past who have left no written record is the way populations distributed themselves over the landscape. An area which shows evidence of concentrated activity is called a site. This can be a spot where a group of hunters trapped and killed a mammoth: a kill site. Or it can be an area of 10 square kilometers containing residences, workshops, palaces, and temples: a city. And it can be anything in between: a camp, a village, a town, or a ceremonial center. What an archaeologist wants to know about a site are its dimensions, its individual areas of activities, whether these activity areas were housed in structures, and how these areas or structures were related to one another. In other words, the archaeologist wants an accurate plan of the site, because this more than any other single piece of information will help him understand how people were living their lives.

More often than not, however, a single site cannot tell the whole story of a community's life. A group of people can use more than one site at the same time. People who rely on hunting as their livelihood can have many kill sites, a quarry site where they get the stone for their tools, and a base camp. And even when life is more complex, perhaps especially when life is more complex, a group of people, while residing in one place, may have important economic, religious, social, and political relationships with other communities at other settlements. Sites that are related to one another in these ways are said to constitute a zone. In very complex societies zones relate to one another, usually through political ties, and then the whole is said to comprise a territory.

Archaeologists are also interested in the number of people occupying an area. The population's size and its density are related to what the environment was like and what technologies the population used to exploit the natural resources. However, the questions are not simply whether the climate permits the cultivation of maize and the community has the digging stick and irrigation canals to grow it. Also important, for example, is whether the technology is successful enough that full-time food producers can support people in the community who do not produce food. The interrelationship of environment, technology, and occupational specialization provides keys to understanding population distributions. Another factor affecting population size and density is diversity of environment. Such variability leads to specialization and then to an interdependent relationship among specialized groups. In Mesoamerica there was enormous diversity and an interdependence from which all profited.

The settled populations of Mesoamerica were at first simple villagers, among whom there seems to have been no specialization of occupation, no one living much better than any one else. The villages apparently were politically autonomous; that is, they do not seem to have had political relationships in which one village was subordinate to another. Later, although the villages continued in many ways unchanged, centers came into existence which may have first been built around temples and the developing religious system. The center and the villages served each other and in doing so created a new social order. The center brought together different communities

21

from different environmental zones and fostered the exchange of products. The people of the villages, in turn, built the centers and supported the priests who could not spend their time producing food.

In other areas the center was a focus not only of religious life but of economic and social life as well. It encompassed more and more individuals, some of whom were food producers but others increasingly were engaged in specialized occupations. Classes became differentiated, both economically and socially. After these centers were established, satellite villages developed to serve the center's needs. In certain situations an entire village specialized in one occupation, and where there were many villages a variety of products was provided for the population of the center. This villages-center arrangement was well-integrated and formed a unified entity which defined the zone. Ultimately some centers expanded beyond the confines of the zone, by means of short military campaigns into uncommitted areas. In this way territories were built up, and finally wars were fought over the right of economic access to territories. Political control over territories came later and was never as important in Mesoamerica as economic dominance. For this reason, territories were never as well integrated as zones.

The architecture at Mesoamerican sites varied according to time and environment. The early villages had rudimentary structures simply because there was no accumulation of architectural knowledge on which to draw. The later cities show how the architects and builders profited from the information handed down to them by their predecessors over hundreds and thousands of years. Architectural change during prehistory does not appear in

all areas of the world, so the spectacular differences between the earlier and the later sites in Mesoamerica
should not be expected or taken for granted. The development of architecture is a special cultural characteristic.

Environment has a profound effect on architecture all
over the world. It governs the kind of protection that is
needed—from storms, hot winds, snow—and it also limits
the choice of building materials. In regions without trees,
for example, even the simplest huts may be made of stone
rather than wood.

The architecture of the different regions of Mesoamerica reflects the attempt to overcome particular problems. Earthquakes, flash floods, wind, the encroaching
tropical vegetation, all produce different architectural results. In regions where earthquakes were known, platforms were well proportioned to support superstructures,
and these were never very high. The walls of buildings
were made of large rock courses alternating with courses
of small stones in a mixture of clay and gravel. The walls
were thus both solid and elastic and able to withstand as
well as to absorb the quakes. The roofs of buildings in
regions with sudden summer downpours have slope for
drainage, even though they follow a general Mesoamerican flat construction, and the sides of walls have special
plaster run-offs to carry the water from the roof to the
ground where a floor drain and a subfloor conduit carried
the water away from the building. In regions where the
sun's rays were so direct that exposure without protection
for more than a few minutes could cause sunstroke, the
doorways and windows were oriented to the west so that
only the cooler late afternoon rays could enter the house.
Where the vegetation was difficult to cut and cleared

23

ground hard to maintain, the platforms had small bases and the superstructures climbed proportionately high above them.

Architects and builders in Mesoamerica, like those elsewhere, used the materials that were easily available to them. In regions where there had been volcanic flows, lava, which is both light in weight and impervious to rain, was a favorite building material. Caliche, a soil layer consisting of calcium carbonate, which can be as hard as stone, was commonly used in those arid and semi-arid regions where it formed. But the principle of "use what is at hand" did not always prevail. Men sometimes journeyed many kilometers to quarries for basalt and andesite which they needed or wanted for their structures. Especially remarkable in Mesoamerica, where the wheel was never invented and no draft animals were available for transport, were the methods by which stones, sometimes weighing up to 200 tons, were moved from the sources to the centers. It took many men and a great deal of time to effect their transport, because the raw human energy was relieved by only the simplest mechanical aids. The larger stones were dragged on sledges and the smaller ones, up to 2 tons, were carried in slings or on litters supported by poles on men's shoulders. In a modern experiment, thirty-five men took a week to carry a 1-ton stone 7 kilometers.

Wood was an important supplementary material in the great buildings. It was used in the construction of the roof (providing the beams, pole laths, and/or planks), in the cores of columns, and for pillars, jambs, lintels, and closures.

Lime was used extensively to make plaster, which covered floors, roofs of buildings, and walls, as well as the

broad open plaza areas. In some areas caliche was pro-
cessed to make plaster which was employed for the same
purposes.

The houses of the village people were simple. They
were made of wood, stone, cane, and mud and very often
had thatched roofs. Because, compared to the great stone
edifices, houses of this kind disintegrate easily, archaeologists have had little direct evidence of them. The native
pre-Hispanic pictorial documents and some pottery vessels
depicted village houses, and archaeologists have used
these sources in their reconstructions.

The artifacts most common in Mesoamerica were ceramic vessels. Millions of them were made, and since
fired clay is easily preserved under almost any climatic
conditions, they are important sources of study. Archaeol-

Ceramic vessel in the shape of a dog, from the state of Colima in Western Mexico. The ware was red-slipped and highly polished. The dog
portrayed is a kind that was raised for food. It was considered a deli-
cacy by the Aztecs, and such ceramics as this, as well as surviving
bones, indicate that these dogs were eaten in Mesoamerica much earlier. Other vessels from Colima portray animals, such as parrots, peli-
cans, armadillos, and some human figures with distinctive features
suggesting they were representations of specific persons.

Fragment of a vessel from the Mayan area, depicting a ceremonial scene, Tikal Museum, Guatemala. The painting is in several colors on a white background. A seated figure presented in a naturalistic style is gesturing as he speaks to others not visible in this view. These vessels commonly show glyphs which date and elucidate the scene.

ogists are interested in ceramic vessels because they can be used for demarcating chronological periods, for showing relationships among different regions, and for describing the content of a culture.

The makers of ceramic vessels change their ideas from

time to time about how they should manufacture and decorate their products. They choose different clay sources, invent new shapes, and appreciate fresh decorative motifs. Change is an indication that time has passed, and archaeologists use change in ceramics to measure time. Chronological periods are defined on the basis of the appearance and disappearance or shift in frequencies of ceramic types or characteristics.

Quite often potters are inspired by the work of other potters and borrow their techniques and designs. Similarities in ceramics from different regions indicate that the populations have been in contact with one another. Perhaps they have been trading, or perhaps a group has migrated from one place to the other.

The vessels themselves show a great deal about what life was like within a community. First, they reveal something about technology. For example, the marks on the

Roll-out of the drawing on a circular Mayan vessel, University of Pennsylvania Museum, Philadelphia. The procession shown is headed by an exalted personage borne in a litter, who is followed by a bearer and then by men wearing elaborate headdresses similar to the leader's. The drawing has no geometric perspective and the style is stiff, but the lack of naturalism contributes to the ritualistic quality of the scene.

vessels made in Mesoamerica show that no potter's wheel was used there; vessels were either shaped by hand out of coils, lumps, or patches of clay or were made in molds. As elsewhere, shapes were created to serve specific purposes. Neckless bowls held seeds, tall jars with constricted necks carried water, and flat plates were used to cook tortillas. The presence of elaborately decorated vessels in some graves and plain ware in others is a clue to differentiation of social classes. Some notion of religion and ideology can come from a study of the symbols used to decorate the vessels.

In order to get this information the archaeologist must analyze a ceramic collection according to a standard list of characteristics. These characteristics include the nature of the paste, particularly its texture and color; the way the vessel was made, whether by hand or mold or a combination of both; how the surface was finished—whether it was merely wiped with a rag or polished to a luster with a small stone; the color of the slip (the thin solution of clay and water which gives the vessel a different color from the paste and also renders it impermeable to water); the shape of the vessel; the decorative technique—incised, molded, appliquéd, painted; and the decorative motif.

Ceramics as an industry developed in Mesoamerica in the third millennium B.C. Many kinds of decorative as well as utilitarian objects were made of pottery. Next to vessels perhaps the most popular items were figurines. These were small and large, of men, women, animals, and houses. They were handmade, molded, incised, appliquéd, and painted. They too have yielded a great deal of information about chronology and spatial relationships. Other clay products were spindle whorls used in spinning thread, seals, smoking pipes, and musical instruments.

Typical ceramic figurines depicting daily life. The woman, at right, wears a plain skirt and head covering, with only earrings for ornamentation, and is dressing her hair. The man, clad simply in a breechclout and cap, appears to be talking between sips from his cup. Such figurines, despite their commonplace subjects, were made as funeral offerings and were buried with the dead.

Handmade and painted ceramic figures of musicians, from western Mexico. In this pair of figures, the one on the left holds a deeply incised bone, which he scrapes with a tool that made a rasping sound. The other, under his crescent-shaped nose ornament, blows into a flute resting on a vessel that served as a resonator.

Ceramic figurines in Preclassic style. These figurines, ranging from 8 to 30 centimeters in height, have been grouped to show variations in the depiction of the human form in the Preclassic period. Despite the differences, they show some common characteristics. The torsos and appendages are roughly formed and the genitals eliminated, but the head was modeled with care and the facial features show attention to detail. All the figures have elaborate hairdos or headdresses and ear ornaments. The two-headed figure (*lower left*) was probably intended to symbolize the idea of duality, important in the Mesoamerican world.

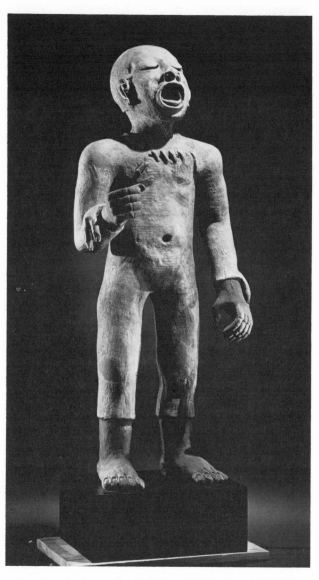

Ceramic figurine representing a priest of the cult of the god of spring, Xipe Totéc, "Our Lord the Flayed One," National Museum of Anthropology, Mexico City. In the ritual of the cult a sacrificial victim was killed and then flayed. The priest dressed himself in the skin to symbolize new vegetation covering the winter earth in spring. In this example, the limp hands of the victim hang over the priest's viable ones, and the priest's mouth sings a prayer from behind dead lips.

Ceramic figurine of a type often found in Nayarit. These are usually between 30 and 60 centimeters high, hollow, and finely finished. The legs and buttocks are emphasized to the point of caricature and the arms so foreshortened that they suggest deformity. Careful attention is given to hairdos and decorative jewelry through techniques of modeling and incising. The woman here wears armlets and a broad necklace, and her ears are pierced several times along the rims and hoops looped through the holes. This style of ear ornament is unusual; most people in Mesoamerica wore a single ear plug in each ear.

In contrast to pottery making, stone working is a more ancient art, used throughout the prehistory of Mesoamerica. Stone tools were manufactured by a number of techniques. The earliest and most persistent one was percussion flaking, in which a rough shape was fashioned by hammers of stone, bone, antler, or wood. Only certain kinds of rocks can be made into tools. They must be hard, homogeneous, and have no natural planes of cleavage, so that a sharp blow will create a fracture where the knapper (stone worker) wants it, instead of along a plane inherent in the rock. Obsidian and chert were commonly chosen for stone tools.

A knapper used hammers to chip flakes off the core. Sometimes the flakes were used, with or without further

Spear point, about 10 centimeters long, from the Mixteca-Puebla site of Tepexi el Viejo in Puebla, Pueblan Institute of Anthropology and History. The larger scars on the face are the result of percussion flaking and the smaller scars along the edges are the product of pressure flaking.

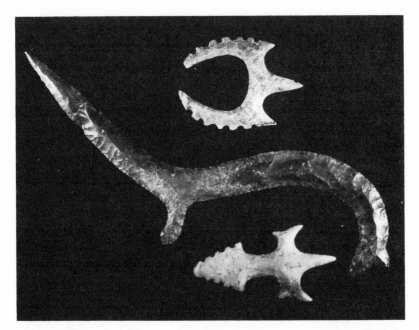

Classic Mayan flint tools, chipped by percussion and pressure techniques, Collection of the American Museum of Natural History, New York. These oddly shaped tools, the epitome of the stone knapper's skill, have sometimes been called "eccentrics," because neither ethnohistorical research nor experimental archaeology has satisfactorily determined their use. The large tool in the center is 42 centimeters long.

modification, as the tool and sometimes the core was worked on further to make a particular tool. Modification—that is, the finer work of shaping and edging a tool—was done by a pressure technique in which small pieces of stone were pressed from the surface of the core or flake with a small stone or piece of bone, wood, or antler.

These techniques are all called chipping. Two other techniques are grinding and polishing. Fine-grained igneous rocks, such as basalt, nephrite, and serpentine, lend themselves to grinding and polishing, by which a smooth and lustrous finish is produced. Other stones, such as limestone, lava, and granite, were also shaped by grinding to form mortars and pestles and slabs on which maize and other vegetables were crushed.

35

Stone figurine from Guerrero in the Mezcala River basin. About 20 centimeters high, it exemplifies the simplicity and expressiveness of the Mezcala style of objects fashioned from a hard stone which takes on a high luster when polished. The stoneworker began with a basic flower-petal shape (often the shape of ceremonial axes) and modified it by incising, grinding, and polishing. Despite the economical use of cuts and planes, he succeeded in conveying not only the sense of the head and body but the mood of the figure as well.

LEGACY FROM PREHISTORIC TIMES

Archaeologists use stone tools, as they do ceramics, to learn about spatial relationships, chronology, and activities. Did the rock come from a distant source for example? Sometimes the form of a tool, such as an arrowhead, has been standardized in one region and adopted by another. As men developed more efficient procedures, later tools were made differently from earlier ones. Thus, material, style, and manufacturing techniques yield information on time and space, and these characteristics are used in describing and analyzing stone tools.

Stone tools have many more forms and purposes than pottery and are therefore a richer source in reconstructing activities. Axes, projectile points, cutting implements, drills, awls, gouges, pounders, mortars and pestles, blades, and a hundred other implements tell how men managed to get their food, clothe themselves, build their houses, and conquer empires.

Mezcala-style votive temple. Although the best-known creations in this style are figures of humans and animals, small votive temples (7 to 9 centimeters high) were also made. This example is fairly simple; others show terraces, stairways, and sometimes several stories.

Stone had not only utilitarian but aesthetic uses. It was employed for monumental sculptures and elaborately carved façades of buildings, as well as carved pillars, stelae, altars, accouterments of the ball game, masks, and incense burners. In fine lapidary work jade, obsidian, rock crystal, agate, amethyst, opal, Mexican onyx, turquoise, amber, and jet were fashioned into figures, ear plugs and lip plugs, pendants, and beads, among other objects.

Metal objects were not common in Mesoamerica, partly because metallurgy was not well known until late in prehistory and partly because it was never a widely used technology. Some utilitarian objects, such as axes, adzes, chisels, fishhooks, awls, and tweezers, were made of metal, but it was used for the most part in the manufacture of decorative items such as statuettes, masks, helmets, diadems, bells, beads, ear and lip plugs, nose ornaments, and others. The metals used were primarily gold, silver, and copper, but tin, lead, bronze (an alloy of copper and tin), and tumbaga (an alloy of copper and gold) were also worked.

Many metallurgical techniques were employed: hammering (either in a cold or hot state), lost-wax casting, gilding, fusing, and soldering. Artisans skilled in metal working were brought to the great cities to practice and to teach their art, but it was always a limited and exclusive art form. The products of lapidary and metal work have been analyzed according to style and function. Because they are primarily decorative they have been an important source of information on the content of intellectual and aesthetic life.

There are also other categories of objects. Hundreds of types of artifacts were manufactured of wood, bone, and shell. Baskets, textiles, petroglyphs, pictographs, and

Palma from Veracruz, American Museum of Natural History, New York. Palmas, so called because the shape is like a palm leaf, range in height from 15 to 80 centimeters, are notched at the top, and have a concave surface at the base, perhaps made to fit against a curved edge. These characteristics and the fact that palmas cannot stand alone have suggested to some archaeologists that the palma was worn with a yoke and was part of the costume of players in the ritual ball game. The back was always undecorated, while the front was carved with representations of animals, humans, or inanimate objects.

Small carved jade head from Tikal in Guatemala, one of the major centers in the Maya area. The face, with typical Mayan features, is clasped between the jaws of a mythical animal, a theme not uncommon in Meso-american art.

mural paintings are numerous. The ancient people of Mesoamerica were prolific, skillful, and inventive craftsmen.

Thus, the archaeological reconstruction of the Meso-american past has rested largely on material remains of the settlement patterns, the architecture, and the ceramic, stone, metal, and other artifacts, seen against the background of the local and regional environment. Material culture is linked to behavior; it is the manifestation of behavior. Since behavior is patterned, material culture must be patterned. The discovery and understanding of the patterning of material remains make it possible to reconstruct behavior and ultimately to explain how and why cultures take one form rather than another. Archaeologists working in Mesoamerica have used material remains in just this way. They have discovered them, analyzed their characteristics, related different patternings to one another, and, finally, have drawn the picture of Mesoamerican culture from the arrival of man until the impact of the conquest.

40

3

PRELUDE TO CIVILIZATION

MAN evolved in the Old World several million years ago, and he entered the New World probably no more than 40,000 years ago and very likely later than that. He came from Asia to Alaska and eventually migrated down through the North American continent into Central America and finally into South America.

Mexico has yielded very little evidence of this early period. Some data come from Hueyatlaco near Puebla and Tlapacoya near Mexico City. At Hueyatlaco, flakes made into scrapers and projectile points were found in association with the remains of now-extinct Ice Age animals: mammoth, mastodon, camelid, native horse, and four-horned antelope. This evidence seems to point to man as

41

a hunter of big game. At Tlapacoya, tools of andesite were found with piles of animal bones, among them deer and bear. Hueyatlaco is dated around 20,000 B.C. and Tlapacoya around 24,000 B.C.

The most important single find, probably dating from 10,000 B.C., but perhaps as early as 14,000 B.C., is part of the spinal column of a camelid carved to represent the head of an animal. It was found in the Valley of Mexico, along with some stone implements, including a miniature all-purpose cutting-pounding tool. These artifacts are not numerous or varied enough to tell archaeologists much about how men were living at that time.

At Santa Isabel Iztapan in the Valley of Mexico imperial-mammoth bones and projectile points were found together in geological deposits which were dated between 8000 and 7000 B.C. At Tepexpan, a site not far from Santa Isabel Iztapan, in geological deposits of the same date, was found the skeleton of a woman about thirty years old. A careful study of the bones indicated that the woman was in no way different in physical type from present-day Indians in Mexico. These findings indicate that at the end of the Ice Age mammoths, which had died out in North and South America, continued to survive in the Valley of Mexico and were hunted in much the same way as they had been earlier, and that the hunters were of a modern physical type.

In other parts of Mexico, however, other modes of life were flourishing at the same time, and these lifeways continued longer, largely because they were not based on the hunting of the large animals of the Ice Age.

Some of these other lifeways have been described by Richard S. MacNeish of the R. S. Peabody Foundation, who has traced changes in culture over long periods, working chiefly in Tamaulipas and in the Tehuacan Valley and using scattered data from other areas. At Tehuacan in the period dated 10,000–6700 B.C. he found bones of horses and antelope in the bottom layers and, in higher layers, bones of jack rabbits, gophers, rats, turtles, and birds and plant remains, such as fruits, pods, seeds, and leaves. The stone tools included projectile points, choppers, crude blades, scrapers, gravers, scraper-knives, and spokeshaves (specialized notched scrapers used for shaping shafts). The sites were all small, never larger than 100 square meters, and were scattered over the area, not clustered.

From these data MacNeish attempted to reconstruct the patterns of life during that period. At first the people were engaged primarily in hunting activities, using the points to kill game and the scrapers, gravers, and knives to prepare the hides. At the same time they were learning about vegetable foods—which were edible and at what seasons they could be harvested. The choppers and blades were used for harvesting and processing these foods. The small size of the sites indicates that they were occupied by no more than three families or fifteen individuals; in other words, by "microbands." The sites showed only a shallow accumulation of occupational debris, indicating that the microbands did not live there permanently. The similarity of the stone tools from site to site showed that the same microband was occupying more than one site, suggesting that the bands were nomadic. The distribution of the sites gave no indication that territory was delimited, nor did the sites appear to have been occupied seasonally.

As the Ice Age began to wane, the climatic changes affected the flora, in particular by reducing the grasslands where the herd animals roamed. This meant that there

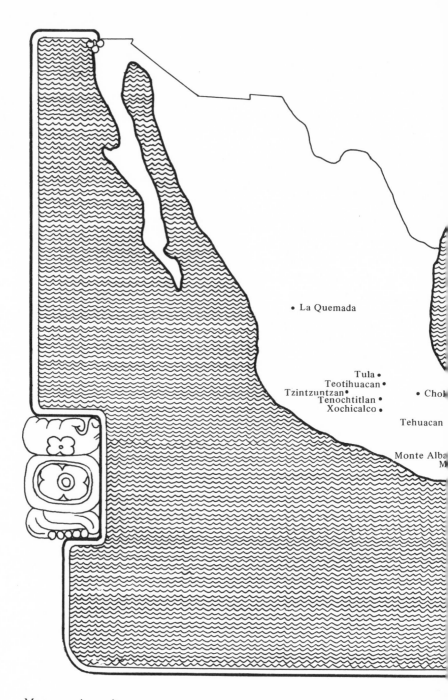

La Quemada

Tula
Teotihuacan
Tzintzuntzan
Tenochtitlan
Xochicalco

Chol

Tehuacan

Monte Alba
M

Mesoamerican sites

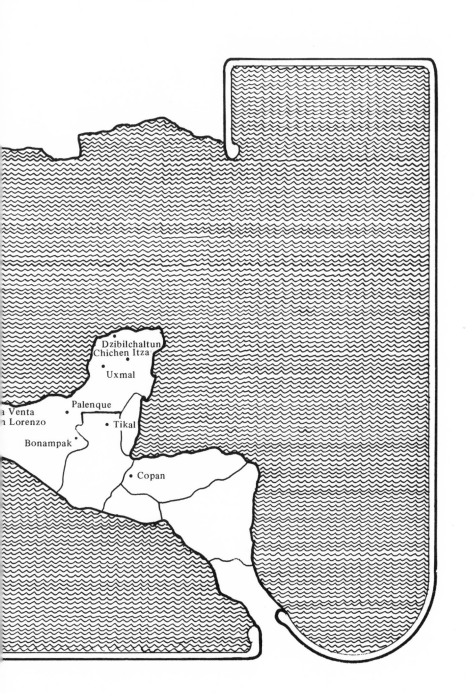

were fewer animals available throughout the year, and consequently the other foodstuffs became increasingly important.

From 6700 through 5000 B.C. another pattern emerged. Excavation revealed that some sites were occupied by small groups, others by many people. A study of the distribution showed that the sites were confined to a limited territory and were clustered in different micro-environments which were revealed by plant and animal remains. The tools found were projectile points (but of a different form from those made previously), choppers and scrapers (made differently from earlier types), gouges, and crude blades. Other stone tools made by grinding rather than chipping were discovered. These included mortars, pestles, milling stones, and mullers (egg-shaped pulverizing implements). Wooden tools now appeared, as well as baskets, nets, mats, and string. Group burials and evidence of cremation, infanticide, and human sacrifice were uncovered.

From this evidence it appears that small groups of people were moving within a designated territory of small environmental niches in a seasonal round. The seasons determined the schedule for acquiring food. In fall the groups picked fruit, cultivated avocados, hunted, and cut leaves. In winter they obtained most of their food by hunting. In spring they collected seeds, picked pods, and also did some hunting and leaf-cutting. In summer the microbands coalesced into larger groups ("macrobands," defined as "a series of microbands") which continued all the spring activities and added the cultivation of mixta squash, amaranth, and chile.

The tools show improved techniques of manufacture, and their varied functions indicate that both hunting and the gathering of plants were major subsistence activities. The introduction of baskets for collecting seeds and pods and of mortars and pestles, milling stones, and mullers for processing them, indicate a shift in the proportions of foods used, to which organic remains also testify. Now only a little more than half the diet (54 percent) was meat, 40 percent came from wild vegetal foods, and 6 percent was produced by cultivation.

The burial practices reveal that rituals concerning death were being developed and indeed foretell some that became part of the Mesoamerican culture pattern. Human sacrifice, for example, became the symbol of social solidarity and, ironically, a mechanism for maintaining populations at survival levels.

Study of the plant and animal remains from the next period—5000–3700 B.C.—shows not so much an abrupt change as a gradual move from nearly equal reliance on game and plants to an increased dependence on the latter. At this time wild plants composed 52 percent of the diet; agricultural produce had risen to 14 percent; and meat declined to 34 percent. This change was accomplished by an improved but essentially similar seasonal round. In stone technology, the changes were slight. Tools which had been formed by percussion were finished with a fine pressure technique, and there were a few new types of projectile points, as well as some new kinds of tools made of wood and bone. In other words, during this period the framework of cultural life was not undergoing radical change, but significant shifts were taking place in scheduling and priorities.

In the next millennium further results of this transposition can be seen. Agricultural produce comprised at least 25 percent of the diet; meat dropped to 25 percent and wild plant foods to 50 percent. Study of the sites and their distribution shows that this was accomplished by increased horticultural activities in the summer and spring. The population gathered together in macroband camps or hamlets which were permanent bases in the spring, summer, and even into the fall months. In the later fall and the winter the macrobands broke up and their members moved into hunting and gathering areas which could be exploited most profitably by small groups.

The stone industry shows an increase in the kinds of implements used for preparing the wild and cultivated vegetal foods. Metates, manos, pestles, and mortars were made in many shapes. The appearance of paint palettes and polishing pebbles for ceramics shows that in this millennium the subsistence basis for a settled as opposed to a nomadic way of life was being established.

Very little is known about the succeeding 1000 years, but by 1500 B.C. a new pattern had become entrenched. In that interim populations shifted from cultivating many plants to growing a few intensively. These were maize, chile, beans, and squash, and they were extremely productive. The sites were occupied very nearly all year round, a result, it would seem, of the fact that the crops were large enough to sustain the population through the late fall and part of the winter. The distribution of the hamlets shows a pattern of clustering—that is, several hamlets were in a zone which formed a larger community. Political relations developed among the various zonal communities.

The technology also reflects a more settled way of life. A major ceramic industry which produced vessels and figurines was under way. Weaving became important, and thread was spun by spindle whorls and cloth was woven on looms.

Burial rituals became more elaborate. The grave was a special deep bell-shaped pit. The body was accompanied by figurines which seem to have been religious objects.

What the material remains from the end of the Ice Age until about 1500 B.C. show is a developing technology and a subsistence pattern that fostered continuing changes in the organization of society. Throughout the year small groups of nomadic peoples were moving, or perhaps more accurately being driven, from one environmental niche to another. They were enabled, through increasing technological control over their environment, to increase their numbers and realign their relationships. By 1500 B.C. small communities whose members had an almost continuous face-to-face association were combining to form more complex social and political units. These critical changes in the organization of society were the basis for further technological change and for the social and political developments which characterize complex societies.

4

PATTERNS TAKE SHAPE

NEITHER in the period just described nor at any other time in its history did Mesoamerica show a uniform cultural development. Different environmental and social causes led to varying degrees and types of change. However, when there was a cultural leap forward in one region, profound reverberations affected others in contact with it. This seems to have been what occurred in the coastal plain of southern Veracruz and northern Tabasco sometime after 1500 B.C.

In this region, which covers an area of perhaps 10,000 square kilometers, an extraordinary development, now called the Olmec culture, emerged. The artifacts of this culture exhibit distinctive characteristics. Art objects

Olmec stone head from San Lorenzo, one of a type distinctively characteristic of that culture. So far fifteen of these sculptures have been
found: four at La Venta, two at Tres Zapotes, eight at San Lorenzo, and
one at Cerro el Vigía. As much as 3 meters high, they seem to have
been associated with the architecture of the centers, and a number of
archaeologists have speculated as to their function; it may have been to
honor dead leaders.

made of stone are of two categories: monumental and portable. The monumental objects were colossal heads made of basalt, as much as 3 meters high and 10,000 kilograms or more in weight; stelae of granite carved in low relief; large, rectangular, elaborately carved block altars; and great stone figures sculptured in the round. The portable art is represented mainly by figures, plaques, pectorals, axes, and celts. The materials most commonly used were a bluish jade, dull green serpentine, and black basalt, although other minerals and wood also served. There were in addition pottery figures, both hollow and solid, and vessels, mainly flat-bottomed bowls with sides that were either vertical or slanted outward.

The most common representation in Olmec art is the were-jaguar, a creature which combines the characteristics of a jaguar and a human baby. The head is cleft; the eyes are narrow or oval; the nose is flat. The mouth is usually open, revealing toothless gums or sometimes two long feline eyeteeth, and the corners are turned down in a baby's cry or an animal's snarl. The body has the plumpness of an infant and lacks sexual organs.

A customary explanation for this were-jaguar motif draws on a myth for which there is support in one or two items of sculpture: a jaguar is said to have copulated with a woman in the remote past and produced a race of were-jaguars. Another interpretation, however, has been offered by Peter Furst, an ethnologist at the State University in Albany, N.Y. Furst made a study of myths concerning jaguars throughout Latin America and found that there was a special relationship between jaguars and shamans (practitioners of magic and ritual). Shamans are seen as capable of transforming themselves into jaguars and taking on their physical and behavioral characteristics, and jaguars (especially those who attack humans) are thought to be transformed shamans. Is it this transformation which the Olmec were trying to represent in their were-jaguar figures?

Furst's findings indicated that various narcotics were used to induce the transformation. The drugs released the jaguar in the shaman or permitted him to feel and act as

Hollow ceramic figurine in the Olmec style from Puebla, about 30 centimeters high, Museum of Primitive Art, New York. Hollow figurines are far more difficult to form and fire than solid ones. This figure is covered with a white slip, which highlights the form and surface details. The back was painted in red to suggest that the body was painted or tattooed. The plump arms and legs, protruding stomach, and fat breasts of this and similar figures have suggested to some archaeologists that they are meant to represent babies, to others that they depict eunuchs.

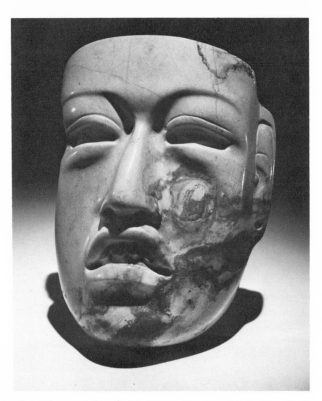

Jadeite mask in the Olmec style, about 13 centimeters high. The lapidaries preferred certain colors of this hard semiprecious stone, particularly translucent blue-green and emerald green. The mask combines the features of man and jaguar in the long, slanting eyes, and more particularly in the mouth which appears to be both snarling and crying.

his jaguar alter ego. An examination of Olmec artifacts revealed a number of spoons and snuffing tubes which could have been used for ingesting narcotics. This function seems to be indicated by the use of bird forms in the design or decoration of the implements, since birds are regarded as spirits or patrons of intoxication. Furst found some Olmec spoons and snuffers with representations of both jaguars and birds.

Furst believed that the sexlessness of the were-jaguar figures might also be related to the ritual of transformation. The shaman was commonly required to observe

54

certain rules of sexual abstinence in order to have the physical and psychological fortitude to undergo the transformation. Sexlessness would then refer, not to a physical state, but rather to the behavior of the shaman.

The Olmec sites which comprise the "heartland" of Olmec culture lie on the coastal plain between the Gulf of Mexico and the Tuxtla mountains. The land is low, rising not more than 90 meters above sea level, and it is divided by rivers which begin as clear, rapid streams in the mountains, become muddy and sluggish in the flat plain, and end in swamps and lagoons. While the rivers were an important source of food, providing fish, shellfish, turtles, and water fowl, they were a hindrance to the expansion of agriculture. The rain, which ranges from 185 to 310 centimeters annually, falls chiefly in the summer months, and the turgid rivers then overflow and flood the savannas. Without methods to prevent flooding and permit drainage,

Olmec-style stone figurine about 10 centimeters high, National Museum of Anthropology, Mexico City. This type of figurine is characterized by a body stance in which the arms hang down the sides, the knees bend slightly, and the body leans gently forward. While the figure is nude and appears to be that of a man, no genitals are shown. The face has the characteristics of a were-jaguar, and the head is deformed, a common practice among Mesoamerican peoples, who bound the heads of infants at an age when the skull was still malleable.

the river land could not be used for cultivation. In addition, some of the rest of the land is swampy and would be unsuitable for crops even when it was not subject to flooding.

Thus, the land best suited for cultivation was the area of tall jungle vegetation. It has been suggested, on the basis of present-day farming practices in the area, that the land was cleared by a slash-and-burn method. In this technique the vegetation is cut by stone tools in March; in May, the driest month, the cut vegetation is burned, and the field is cleared and made ready for planting in June.

The soil quickly becomes exhausted and after a few years the plots must be allowed to return to jungle growth. The result is that, for every cultivated acre, five lie fallow. Even though some cultivated areas can yield two crops a year, the main one in December and a smaller harvest at the end of May, this type of agriculture cannot support large dense populations. The proportion of worked to fallow acreage means that only 17 percent of the land is being used at any time. If the population grows, some people must go greater distances to cultivate the land. In other words, what follows from this method of cultivation is a dispersed distribution of population. The two earliest Olmec sites now known, San Lorenzo and La Venta, both show the pattern of a small ceremonial center without any significant population, supported apparently by peoples in the hinterlands. La Venta, for example, probably had about 150 residents, but it had a support area of some 600 square kilometers, which, it is estimated on the basis of farming practices just described, could have sustained a population of 18,000.

San Lorenzo and La Venta are the base sites of the Olmec heartland. San Lorenzo is important for two reasons: it provides the longest chronological sequence, including a pre-Olmec period, and it yields the earliest dates for the Olmec. The site, located in the Coatzalcoalcos River basin in southern Veracruz, was first occupied about 1500 BC. At this time there was an established settlement with an important ceramic industry. Within 200 years an enormous amount of construction was undertaken. The plateau on which the site stood was built up by many artificial ridges. Between 1250 and 700 B.C. San Lorenzo became an Olmec site—that is, the artifacts dated to that period exhibit the characteristics which have defined the Olmec culture. The site consisted of 200 house mounds, rectangular courts, and pyramids. The structures are set along a north-south axis. Further excavation is expected to reveal a ball court among the structures. Besides the main grouping, there are other house mounds clustered around small courts. The population residing at the site is estimated to have been no more than 1000 at its maximum. Drainage systems and reservoirs found in the environs of the site were clearly a response to the heavy seasonal rainfall.

Many huge stone monuments—colossal heads, altars, figures, and stelae—have been found at San Lorenzo. Except for one altar of schist, they are all made of basalt, though the nearest basalt source is 60 kilometers away. It is presumed that the Olmec builders brought the basalt from the quarry to the upper Calzadas River and floated it on great log rafts to the Coatzalcoalcos River near the site. From the river bank the stone would have to have been hauled some 50 meters to the site itself.

Sometime between 900 and 700 B.C. these monuments were mutilated. The faces of the figures were smashed, the heads knocked off, the bodies slashed with axes, and

57

the figures buried under mounds of earth. Later a new ceramic industry appeared and Olmec traits were no longer found. The implication is that an immigrant people took over the community. In any case, the settlement never regained its earlier magnificence.

A second significant Olmec site, La Venta, in Tabasco, was partly contemporary with San Lorenzo, and after San Lorenzo had been taken over by invaders, La Venta became the most important Olmec center. Its earliest dates are around 1200 B.C., and the Olmec tradition may have continued there as late as 400 B.C.

La Venta is on an island about 3.5 square kilometers in area, which lies in a coastal swamp. The site is laid out in a 3-kilometer-long line which runs in an approximately north-south direction. There is a central massive structure, about 30 meters high, in the shape of a fluted cone. To the north of this are two long low mounds enclosing a courtyard containing two smaller and shorter rectangular mounds, and beyond this complex is a plaza with 3-meter-high basalt columns set in an adobe wall. There are also three massive mosaic pavements at the site. Each was made of 485 blocks of green serpentine filled in with colored clays or sands and representing jaguar masks. The mosaics were buried, which has suggested to archaeologists that they were constructed as a religious offering. Other massive offerings were layers of blocks of serpentine which were placed at the bottom of deep pits and then buried under mounds of earth.

Perhaps the most touching offering buried at La Venta is one consisting of twenty-two small objects arranged in a scene. Six celts or ax heads form the backdrop, in front of which stand sixteen figurines, one of which is made of a coarser stone than the others. All the figures are were-jaguars. Is the scene meant to convey a ritual message to the forces to whom it was offered? The emotions of group confrontation and individual isolation are clearly portrayed, but the interpretation still eludes archaeologists.

The site of La Venta was destroyed about 600 B.C., or perhaps as late as 400 B.C., and, as at San Lorenzo, the monuments were mutilated. However, the site was never forgotten. Even after the Spanish conquest, people came to it, at first to rob it of stone and jade and then to place offerings in what must have remained in the natives' collective memory as a sacred place.

The Olmec culture was the most complex in Mesoamerica up to this time. The settlements included habitation hamlets in addition to the great centers. Although the centers had some dwellings, they were essentially built for other purposes, apparently for religious and public or civic functions. The number of industries indicates a division of tasks. Farming was carried on, and at the same time centers were being built, monuments carved, ceramics manufactured. Some people may have been released from food-producing tasks and engaged exclusively in manufacturing craft products. Perhaps, too, there was an elite directing religious and civic work at the centers. Some stelae show figures with elaborate headdresses talking to men without such adornments. The former may represent those individuals who held a special place in the social system because of their activities at the centers. In other words, there seems to have been a pattern of social differentiation and occupational specialization which has not been found earlier.

Olmec influence was widespread in Mesoamerica. At certain sites in northern and central Veracruz, for example, Olmec figurines and ceramic vessels are found among artifacts of the local culture. At other sites, on the coast and in the highlands of Chiapas, Oaxaca, central Veracruz, Puebla, Morelos, the Valley of Mexico, and Guerrero, excavated artifacts appear to be a blend of local and Olmec styles. While archaeologists are not sure of all the reasons for the presence of the Olmec style outside its heartland, the distribution of Olmec artifacts and traits throughout Mesoamerica has been considered an indica-

The group of figurines and ceremonial axes found at La Venta, National Museum of Anthropology, Mexico City. The six axes and fifteen of the figurines are made of jade and serpentine. The sixteenth figurine, standing against the backdrop of axes, is made of sandstone.

tion of Olmec ability to exploit different environmental zones for products lacking in its own. This capability came from the fabric of Olmec society itself and is based on social and economic differentiation. As work in the Valley of Oaxaca by Kent Flannery, a University of Michigan archaeologist, has suggested, the exchange of goods was between the elites of the Olmec and other societies, not among the ordinary people. The other societies were

The figures are about 18 centimeters high. The excavators of this cache discovered that, some time after the pieces had been buried, another hole was dug as though later people wanted to view them again or to make sure they were still there.

in the highlands, where food supply was actually or potentially more secure than in the Olmec lowlands. The exchange of exotic materials—such as highland magnetite on the one side and coastal marine shell on the other—for the manufacture of luxury goods may have developed in order to establish the means by which foodstuffs could move from the agriculturally successful highlands to the somewhat precariously cultivated lowlands.

Since the Olmec seem to have been most successful in exchanges with societies that had emerging or established elites, they would have endeavored to stimulate or reinforce the presence of such groups. The later importance of social classes in the valleys of Oaxaca and Mexico can surely be traced in part to encouragement by the Olmec.

The Olmec also created the framework for what William Sanders of Pennsylvania State University, an archaeologist interested in ecological studies, has called an inter-regional symbiotic network. Such a network developed from reciprocal trading among units with differing climates producing different kinds of goods. The contact forced communities into situations that were unknown when they were in isolation; they came to know dependency, interaction, and negotiation. In time special institutions came into being as a response to the need for mediation among interrelated communities, but the idea of making intercommunity relations a source for community development was fashioned by the Olmec.

The Olmec legacy to Mesoamerica was social stratification and a system of economic exchange. The next millennium saw the flowering of varied complex societies which sprang from Olmec seeds but, taking root in different soils and experiencing different nurturing, had different forms.

5

THE FIRST GREAT CENTERS

MESOAMERICA is divided into innumerable microenvironmental zones. They are highly diverse and great differences can be found within a few kilometers. These zones, sometimes altered by critical technological devices such as irrigation, produced a wide range of products which circulated throughout the entire Mesoamerican region. The interchange led to more effective utilization of the environments, to increased specialization, and finally to an institutionalized interdependence of local populations. The period between A.D. 250 and 600 was a time of interdependence among local regions and a resultant complexity of particular societies as they emerged on a high level of organization. In southern Mexico two major centers arose: Teotihuacan in the Valley of Mexico and Monte Albán in the Valley of Oaxaca.

TEOTIHUACAN—HUB OF COMMERCE

THE site of Teotihuacan lies in the subvalley of the same name in the Valley of Mexico and represents the single most important settlement in that locality at that time. The development of this great city with its large, dense population did not result from population movements into the Valley of Mexico from other areas of Mesoamerica, but rather from a population shift between 150 and 1 B.C. from other zones of the Valley of Mexico into the subvalley.

William Sanders has studied the settlement patterns in the Teotihuacan subvalley from 1000 B.C. onward and has traced the changes which culminated in the establishment of the Teotihuacan culture. Between A.D. 1 and 150 ceremonial architecture appeared for the first time in the subvalley, and with it emerged what Sanders calls "site stratification"—indications of differences in rank among a number of contemporary settlements exemplified by variations in size, kinds of structures, craft products, and burials. Sanders's work has shown that at first the subvalley was divided into a number of small competing zones, each comprising a small hilltop town or village and dependent hamlets. These settlements began moving from the hilltops to the valley floor and a sizable percentage of the population was united into the single settlement of Teotihuacan. It was characterized early by the development of a nuclear center and by monumental architecture. An analysis of the distribution of artifacts and their relationship to the various structures indicates

64

that the population was differentiated in relation to wealth and social status and that there was also occupational specialization. Teotihuacan became the major population center in the entire Valley of Mexico. Rapid population growth caused more intensive use of land, and centralization of the settlement, social and economic differentiation, and specialization increased.

The heyday of Teotihuacan was between A.D. 250 and 600. A map of the city made in a ten-year project under the direction of University of Rochester archaeologist René Millon shows a maximum area of 20 square kilometers, with a planned nucleus and an outlying district that was largely unplanned. The broad outlines of the city plan may have been conceived in an early master design.

The nucleus was divided into quadrants which were defined by a north-south axis, now called the Street of the Dead, and by an east-west axis, now called East and West avenues. The Street of the Dead, however, extended beyond the nucleus. Most buildings were oriented according to the north-south axis. In the geographic center of the city were two immense enclosures, the Citadel and the Great Compound. A study of their plans and the artifacts associated with them indicates that together these enclosures formed the religious, bureaucratic, and commercial center of the city. Also on the Street of the Dead were two great pyramids: the Pyramid of the Moon and the Pyramid of the Sun. Today they are the two most impressive structures at the site. The Pyramid of the Moon holds a commanding position in the center of the Street of the Dead but is smaller than the Pyramid of the Sun which stands on the eastern side of the Street. Millon has shown that the Pyramid of the Sun was built over a long period of time and completed before A.D. 250. The dates of the construction may be between A.D. 100 and 200.

The main residential area was in the northwest quadrant. This was the oldest part of the city and bordered on land unsuited for cultivation. Other areas also contained residences. Teotihuacan was divided into neighborhoods, or *barrios*. Some *barrios* contained groups of buildings in which were found artifacts produced by potters, obsidian knappers, and lapidaries. More than 500 workshops were found, and it is estimated that 25 percent of the population was engaged in craft production. Excavators also

Teotihuacan in the Valley of Mexico, aerial view. The nucleus of the city was bisected by the broad Street of the Dead and contained such monumental structures as the Pyramid of the Sun, as well as public buildings, private residences, and places of business.

found the houses of the farmers who worked the rich land on the southwestern and eastern perimeters of the city. Goods from outlying regions discovered in market areas seem to show that long-distance trade was carried on. The public buildings and elaborate residences point to the existence of a religious and political elite.

In calculating the size of the population Millon used data on the sleeping rooms of apartment compounds throughout the site. He arrived at a minimum population of 75,000 and a probable population of 125,000 for the city at its height. The growth of the population has been tied to its economic development. The earlier pattern of trade between Teotihuacan and other regions was supplemented by the production of goods within the city, thus adding jobs to the economy which supported an increasing local population and also attracted settlers from outlying areas.

Agricultural productivity was, of course, critical for the expansion of the city's population. It was based on the cultivation of three prolific crops: maize, squash, and beans. More important to its success, however, was the technological innovation of irrigation canals which made possible the cultivation of lands which would have been unproductive if rainfall had been the only source of water.

Teotihuacan must have been a bustling place. Its people represented many occupations: priests, political administrators, traders, craftsmen, and farmers. Its structures reflected the complexity of life, for there were not only residences, lowly and grand, but also palaces, temples, civic buildings, markets, and workshops. But what is most remarkable about Teotihuacan is that for the first time in the history of Mesoamerica all aspects of life were enclosed within one settlement. Mesoamerican society was

67

Street of the Dead, Teotihuacan. Restoration of the center of the city by the Mexican National Institute of Anthropology in the 1960s revealed that the mounds which lined this street did not contain burials as had been supposed but were pyramidal platforms. The Pyramid of the Sun in the background dominates the entire site.

organized differently from the way it had been previously. Teotihuacan represents the ability of men to integrate all parts of society into a single system through new kinds of social and political mechanisms. The ties based on kinship which separated people into groups seem to have been superseded by ties based on function, and the major social division became the one between those who ruled and those who were ruled. It was the ruling bureaucracy which represented the whole community as a political unit.

Beyond the settlement and into the zone, relationships appear to have been more economic than political. Jeffrey Parsons, a University of Michigan archaeologist working

68

on settlement studies, has suggested as a result of his own work in the Valley of Mexico that the Texcoco region may have comprised a rural zone whose population was engaged in a variety of economic activities, such as salt making, fowling, and plant collecting, which were tied to the needs of the inhabitants of Teotihuacan. The small settlements of the Valley of Mexico, however, do not seem to have been integrated into a monolithic Teotihuacan political community. Their specializations provided some measure of political independence even while they tied the people to the economy of the great city.

The Pyramid of the Moon and the Citadel, Teotihuacan. The latter contains the small Temple of Quetzalcoatl, where a sculptured head of a feathered serpent decorates the balustrade; in the background are the walls of the Citadel enclosure and in the distance behind these is the Pyramid of the Moon at the head of the Street of the Dead.

MONTE ALBAN—IN PRAISE OF THE DEAD

WHILE there was no other settlement equal to Teotihuacan in extent, complexity, or population size and density, there was at least one other that may have shown a similar pattern: Monte Albán in the Valley of Oaxaca. Monte Albán is on a hill 2000 meters above sea level. It is at the junction of three valleys which form the larger Valley of Oaxaca. The history of Monte Albán begins between 600 and 300 B.C. when the Great Plaza in the nucleus of the settlement, measuring 200 by 300 meters, was created by leveling and plastering the entire summit of the hill. One of the first buildings was a pyramidal platform, now called the Mound of the Danzantes (Dancers). Its façade was made up of rows of large, irregular, but approximately rectangular stones, on which were engraved nude figures of men whose bodies, particularly the arms and legs, were portrayed in motion. These figures have been called the

(*Left*) The Great Plaza at Monte Albán. Most of the buildings were constructed in the Classic period. Among the architectural features of Classic Monte Albán are the use of ornamental panels on the base as well as on the upper part of stairway balustrades and stairways set into rather than added to the platform. The architectural style of Monte Albán has been thought to reflect the demands of religious life rather than the aesthetic choices of the architects. (*Below*) Carving on the Mound of the Danzantes at Monte Albán.

Dancers, but their nudity has suggested to some that they were warriors, since warriors were commonly depicted stripped of weapons and clothing. The apparently mutilated genitals and the writhing movement of the bodies have also suggested that the figures represent soldiers who had been sacrificed or tortured.

Major construction at Monte Albán took place between A.D. 250 and 600 when the settlement was rebuilt by a people called the Zapotecs. Buildings were made of stone and covered with stucco of various colors. Red, for which ocher was used as the pigment, was most common. The rectangular plaza was surrounded by platforms, pyramids, temples, and a ball court, and two structures were placed in the center. The larger of these has been considered the main altar of the plaza. The center portion of the building had broad stairs leading to a temple which is divided into two parts. On one side, at a slightly lower level, was a temple with a single chamber, which was reached by stairs rising from the plaza. The smaller structure, different from all the others in shape and orientation, was bisected by a vaulted corridor which is open at the top, suggesting to some archaeologists that the structure may have been used as an astronomical observatory.

Death had an important place in the philosophy of Monte Albán culture, and the aesthetic energy of the artisans went into the construction and outfitting of subterranean tombs which were found in different places throughout the site. They were often elaborately planned, with an antechamber and a main chamber with a corbeled vaulted ceiling. The walls of some were covered with hieroglyphs and frescoes depicting men and gods in elaborate costumes. The chambers which were the tombs proper contained sumptuous grave goods. In one were found ear ornaments, figurines, pebbles carved in the shape of human heads, and mosaic plaques made by setting pieces of jade and other stones in a stucco matrix. Perhaps the center's function as a necropolis served to attract large numbers of people, who, having paid homage to the elite dead, stayed to transact business. In this way the religious and aesthetic life facilitated the economic.

The habitations for the resident population of Monte Albán were on small terraces along the hill slopes. Not too much has been learned about the occupations of the population, but simple burials, undecorated pottery, and basic stone tools certainly indicate a different economic and social class from that of the people buried in the grand tombs and accompanied by nonutilitarian, decorative items made of imported stones. While the size and density of the population are now being calculated, the number of habitations has caused archaeologists to predict that Monte Albán had a large enough population to be regarded as a city.

The relationship of Monte Albán to the other settlements in the Valley of Oaxaca has not been determined. It appears to be the only possible city and was certainly the largest of all the valley settlements. Further investigation is being done to discover whether it, like Teotihuacan, was the reservoir into which were drained the resources and population of the surrounding zone.

6

THE MAYA: INTELLECTUALS
AND AESTHETES

AROUND A.D. 300 an extraordinary people rose to promi-
nence in southern Mesoamerica: the Maya. Their society,
especially in the lowlands, was markedly different from
the kind of society that developed in the highland sites of
Teotihuacan and Monte Albán. In those the settlement
pattern has been described as urban—that is, there was a
large, dense population, a nucleus with varying structures, and different kinds of habitations. The Lowland
Maya centers had no nucleus; instead, multiroomed palaces, great pyramids, temples, ball courts, stelae, and
altars were distributed throughout the site. There was no

area of habitation to house a large resident population, but only living quarters for the center's functionaries. House mounds indicate that the population relating to the center was distributed over a territory up to 100 square kilometers in extent.

The urban centers drained off population and resources from the zone around them, but in the Lowland Maya region population and resources were more uniformly distributed among a number of centers of equal size. The typical center had a comparatively small population, which consisted almost entirely of the royalty, the nobility, and the priests. There were only a few craftsmen and possibly servants or retainers. A division between the elite and the common people existed, but since the commoners lived largely outside the center, the division was based on simple and limited economic and social differences. In the highland cities, on the other hand, the community was made up of many occupationally specialized and interdependent groups with gradations in each group's access to wealth.

Nor does there seem to have been in the lowlands the kind of potential for the centralization of political power found in the highlands. In the urban center, because there were many component groups living cheek by jowl, political devices could integrate them into a functioning unit. In the Maya Lowlands the center had, in comparison, intermittent and tangential relationships with its dispersed, unspecialized, albeit supportive population, and no such political mechanisms developed.

The Mayan area is divided into northern, central, and southern portions. The northern consists of Yucatán, Quintana Roo, most of Campeche in Mexico, and the northern part of British Honduras. The central comprises

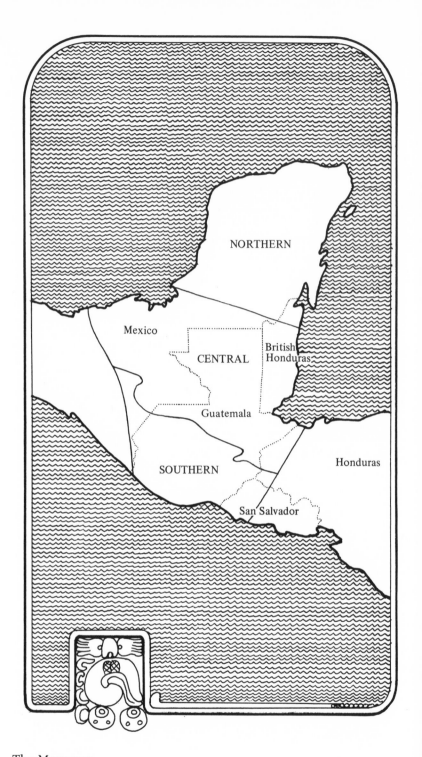

The Maya area

THE MAYA: INTELLECTUALS AND AESTHETES

Petén in Guatemala and parts of the Mexican states of Tabasco and Chiapas. The northern and central portions constitute the Maya Lowlands. The southern area is called the Maya Highlands and consists of the highland regions of Guatemala and Chiapas and the Pacific coastal area of Guatemala and Mexico.

PRE-MAYAN FINDINGS

SOME scattered information has been gathered concerning pre-Mayan culture. Michael Coe of Yale and Kent Flannery of the University of Michigan have shown that in the Pacific littoral of Guatemala near the Chiapas border, in the period between 1500 and 850 B.C., the population was scattered in tiny hamlets (with about twenty individuals in each) which were on the banks of mangrove-lined estuaries and lagoons. The houses were made of wattle and daub and placed on low earthen platforms which were perhaps forerunners of the great platform temples of later times. The remains of oysters, clams, turtles, crabs, fishes, and iguanas and their eggs indicate the bulk of the diet. Maize and the tools for grinding it were also found, suggesting to the investigators that the inland tropical forest, which was suitable for its cultivation, was probably cleared for planting. Pottery and handmade figurines were also discovered, but there is no indication of any sort of craft specialization.

At Dzibilchaltun in northern Yucatán during the period between 800 and 400 B.C. ceremonial architecture began to emerge. An earlier low platform was enlarged and faced with stone, apparently for use in public rituals. Houses were now made of masonry. The data from other sites in the Mayan region dating to this period also reveal a simple village culture with pottery and figurines, the advent of ceremonial structures, and the elaboration of burials.

But there is nothing Mayalike about this village culture, and the antecedents of the distinctive Maya configuration remain to be traced. Michael Coe has suggested that they may be found in the Izapan culture, which is named after the type site of Izapa in the Chiapas highlands. In its art style, dated between 400 B.C. and A.D. 300, he sees motifs which are found commonly in Maya art. Perhaps even more important, Coe has suggested that Olmec influence is clearly discernible in Izapan art and that Mayan culture may be a development from Olmec through Izapan—that is, that Izapan culture may have served as a transition between the Olmec and Mayan focuses.

DISTINGUISHING MAYAN CHARACTERISTICS

MAYAN culture is characterized by distinctive traits of architecture, arts, crafts, and intellectual attainments. Its crystallization has long been considered by archaeologists to have occurred some time in the first millennium of the Christian era in the central portion of the lowland region.

Lowland Maya centers appear to have been built according to a basic plan. The buildings were located around courts and plazas, and the sculptured monolithic monuments, the stelae and altars, were used as adjuncts to the main constructions. Commonly, terraces, platforms, and truncated pyramids were used as substructures to support superstructures which rested on an intermediate building platform. The substructure consisted of a core of rubble and outer walls of masonry and had at least one

Carved stelae at the Maya site of Copán, Honduras. The larger-than-life figures on the stelae stand stiffly under the heavy headdresses and wear their costumes with regal dignity. The deep carving allows for the play of light on the stone emphasizing the embellishments of the costume which contrasts with the figures' bare faces, arms, and legs.

steep stairway either projecting from or inset into it. The superstructure always contained interior space and was roofed by a vault which was created by sloping two masonry walls inward and upward until they met or could be bridged by a capstone. Not infrequently roof combs or crests were carried above the roof line.

Perhaps the major art of the Lowland Maya was the monumental carving exemplified in stelae and altars. The stelae were large, sometimes as high as 3 meters, and were limestone slabs, usually with figures depicted on one side and hieroglyphs on the other. They were set up in the courts of the centers and either commemorated historical or ritual events or served as markers for a calendrical time period. Altars were round or rectangular and have often been found in association with the stelae. Low-relief carvings of lintels and panels and wall paintings were also important art forms.

Ceramic vessels of many forms were produced to serve different purposes. Polychrome pottery was made throughout the period from the fourth to the ninth century A.D. The earlier designs show cranes, flying parrots, and men encircling the vessels. The later vessels have even more brilliant colors, achieved through special firing techniques, and present wonderful narrative scenes.

While ceramic figurines are important throughout the region, probably the most remarkable ones are those found at Jaina, an island off the coast of Campeche. The island contains one of the largest cemeteries known, and the figurines seem to have been manufactured there as grave goods. The greatest number of the figures are of men, whose facial expressions, body stances, and dress are touchingly true to life. In some cases the costumes, although also made of clay, are separate from the figures;

Jaina figurine of a man, National Museum of Anthropology, Mexico City. The exceptionally elaborate costume is completed by a removable headdress. The aggressiveness shown in the face is reinforced by the militant position into which the arms have been moved.

perhaps dressing these forms served some ritual purpose.

Information on the intellectual achievements of the Maya comes from the few surviving native books and from wall paintings, stone sculpture, and ceramic decoration. The interpretation of these is aided by post-conquest accounts of native life. Nevertheless, the reconstructions are only fragmentary since thousands of books and artifacts were either destroyed by zealous Christians determined to convert the heathen or fell as natural prey to time.

The heart of Mayan intellectual life was religion, and their major achievements—writing, numeration, and the calendar—were not only inextricably bound with one an-

81

Figurines from the island of Jaina. In the Mayan cemetery, such figurines, ranging in height from 12 to 25 centimeters, were buried with the dead, as were adornments, ceramic vessels, and utensils. Many of the figures were hand-modeled and painted in blue, yellow, red, green, white, and black. The seated man shows features of the

head and face that were highly regarded by the Maya: the skull is deformed to achieve a high, tapering appearance; the nose forms a line with the forehead; the lines of the mouth are lengthened by scarification. The figurine with the exaggerated but graceful pose (National Museum of Anthropology, Mexico City) has been named "the dancer."

other but also functioned mainly to express the tenets of the religion and to carry out ritual.

Mayan hieroglyphic writing has been studied intensively by J. Eric S. Thompson, an English archaeologist. Thompson's studies have led him to believe that Mayan writing is neither phonemic nor syllabic. Mayan languages that are known historically are largely monosyllabic, and since those of the past seem to have had this character, they could have been conveyed in rebus writing. He concludes that at least some glyphs communicated messages in this way. However, another student of Mayan writing, the Russian ethnologist Yuri Knorosov, believes that the glyphs represent a phonetic-syllabic form of writing. Investigations continue in both these directions.

Most of the glyphs which have been deciphered are simply ideographs. For example, there were glyphs which stood for such basic concepts as sun, moon, directions, and colors. Others were related to the calendar, such as day and month signs. Still others were concerned with deities, and Tatiana Proskouriakoff of Harvard University has suggested that some referred to places and events in the lives of rulers.

There were also number glyphs, but numeration was more commonly expressed through a vigesimal system of position numbers represented by a bar, a dot, and an ellipse. A dot stood for one unit, a bar for five, and the ellipse for zero. The entire position system rests on the idea of zero, and the concept of zero, which the Maya invented independently of the Hindus and the Babylonians, is critical to any mathematical developments beyond simple counting. We do not know how advanced mathematics was among the Maya, but their numeration would cer-

Sculptured hieroglyphic writing on one face of a stela at Copán in Honduras. Glyphs were also incised in stone, carved in wood, modeled in stucco, and painted on pottery, murals, and books.

tainly have permitted them to do arithmetic with ease.

The Mayan calendar was built on an earlier Mesoamerican calendar in which the 260-day cycle formed the basis for all calculations. This earlier calendar was based not only on solar and lunar reckonings but also on an understanding of the related revolutions of the planets. Within the 260-day cycle were 13 units of 20 days each. Running concurrently with the 260-day cycle was a 365-day cycle consisting of 18 units of 20 days each and 5 days at the end. It would take 18,980 days for the two cycles to return to the same numbers and days, and this cycle, of 52 "years," was considered a sacred unit.

While this calendar works excellently to record ongoing time, it floats, in the sense that a date from a beginning point cannot be recorded. The Maya invented a system whereby elapsed time could be noted. A series of units with values in numbers of days were used to express time passed. These were the *kin* (1 day), the *uinal* (20 days), the *tun* (360 days), the *katun* (7200 days), and the *baktun* (144,000 days). According to a correlation of the Christian and Mayan calendars, called the Goodman-Martínez-Thompson correlation after the men who worked on it, the Maya starting date of 13.0.0.0.0. (or 13 baktuns, 0 katuns, 0 tuns, 0 uinal, and 0 kins) corresponds to 3113 B.C. Thus, an early date from the site of Tikal is 8.12.14.8.15 and means that 8 baktuns, 12 katuns, 14 tuns, 8 uinals, and 15 kins had passed since 13.0.0.0.0. The equivalent of the Tikal date in the Christian calendar is A.D. 292.

THE IMPORTANT CENTERS

MOST of the data on the Lowland Maya come from about a dozen ceremonial centers. Among these, the richest

Pyramidal platforms at Tikal, excavated under the auspices of the University of Pennsylvania. Compared to the pyramids of central Mexico, these have narrower bases and proportionately greater heights. In wet, hot climates the growth of vegetation quickly obscures ruins.

yields have been found at Tikal, Copán, Piedras Negras, Palenque, Bonampak, and Uxmal.

Tikal, as a result of the University of Pennsylvania project directed by William Coe of the University Museum, has probably yielded more information than any other single site. The whole of Tikal extended some 64 square kilometers. The main precinct covered an area of 8 square kilometers and contained pyramids, temples, large platforms, altar platforms, and ball courts, which were grouped into complexes and arranged around plazas. This

Pyramidal platform, Tikal, with stelae and altars. This structure, which has been cleared of vegetation, lacks the original facing. Including the roof comb, it is more than 40 meters high. Many stelae have been found at Tikal in plazas and near the stairways of buildings. Some are carved with calendrical glyphs; others, like those here, are uncarved.

precinct also contained elite residences, which could have housed no more than 8,000 people. Most of the population evidently lived outside the main precinct; 5,000 small stone house platforms were found in outlying areas. They are grouped in twos and threes, and in some cases fours, around small patios, and these groupings are in turn clustered on level ridges or natural terraces, apparently to avoid the swampy sandbanks on one side and the steep slopes on the other.

Work at other sites has revealed the architecture and art of the Maya. Copán is noted for its stone sculpture, particularly as seen in the façades of buildings and in altars and

Site of Copán in Honduras (aerial view). The site is on the Copán River, in a valley surrounded by hills. The cleared area in the center is the great plaza containing stelae and altars. The buildings at Copán are made of a greenish volcanic trachyte which harmonizes with the surrounding forests.

stelae. The Temple of the Hieroglyphics has a stairway of sixty-three steps, the risers of which are carved with more than 2,500 glyphs. The elegant ball court with wide sloping sides is perhaps the most famous in Mesoamerica.

The site of Piedras Negras is on a high hill whose elevation was used to give further height to the site. The site is planned around courts, and there are constructions with wide stairways, ball courts, and sweathouses. The style of the exquisitely carved figures in elaborate costumes and the hieroglyphs on wall panels and stelae distinguish Piedras Negras from other sites. The study of these carvings led Tatiana Proskouriakoff to her hypotheses concerning the historical meaning of some Mayan glyphs.

THE MAYA: INTELLECTUALS AND AESTHETES

(*Left*) The ball court at Copán. This court was the third built on this site; two earlier ones were found beneath it. Each of the wide sloping benches which border the playing field is decorated with three parrot heads set in front of the vertical upper wall. Stone masonry courts were introduced in the Classic period, and the ball game seems to have had particular importance in ceremonial life from that time on. It was long-lived and widespread in Mesoamerica, with different versions and meanings in different areas. The ceramic sculpture (*below*) shows the way it was played in Nayarit. The excited spectators crowd the walls while each of the two teams tries to make a goal. The game was played with a heavy rubber ball, which was passed by using only the torso and head.

Palenque, in Chiapas, is a sumptuous site rich in temples. One, the Temple of the Cross, has been investigated intermittently ever since 1785, when official commissions visited the ruins and sent reports to the King of Spain. Probably the most important one is the Temple of the

The Temple of the Cross at Palenque. The sloping upper façade is typical of Palenque temples; at other sites the façade is vertical.

Inscriptions, where Alberto Ruz discovered the funerary crypt of a Mayan ruler. His investigations form one of the heroic adventure stories of Mesoamerican archaeology.

> In choosing the [Temple of the Inscriptions] for the search for a possible inner construction I not only took its size and the importance of its bas-reliefs into consideration, but also the fact that it had never been explored and that its floor instead of being a simple flat stucco surface like in the other buildings was made up of great well-fitted and well-carved slabs which more or less assured inviolability. One of these slabs in the central room caught my attention because it had a double row of perforations, each with a stone plug. On investigating the possible function of this slab I noticed that the walls of the Temple continued below the floor. . . . In fact, excavation revealed not far from the surface a stone that belonged to a vault and further below [an inner stairway].
>
> This stairway had its own perfectly preserved walls and vault, but was completely filled with heavy stone and earth placed there with the intention of obstructing passage. It took us 4 working periods of two and a half or three months each to empty it. The task was rendered even more difficult by the lack of fresh air and the monotony of the work over long periods of time. After a stretch of 45 steps a landing was reached which turned in a U-shape leading into another stretch of 21 steps opening into a passageway. . . .
>
> Finally at the end of the passageway we came to a great triangular slab placed in a vertical position to

The Temple of the Inscriptions at Palenque. The stairway leads from a rear room in the temple across the pyramidal platform to the burial crypt, which is partly below ground level. The stairway had been filled in with rubble to prevent descent and perhaps to disguise the passageway. Covering the sarcophagus in the crypt was a large, elaborately carved stone (*facing page*), weighing 5 tons. Since such a heavy lid could not have been brought down the narrow stairway which led from the temple to the crypt, it has been surmised that the crypt was built earlier. Inside the crypt were masonry supports on which the lid rested before it was slipped into place over the sarcophagus.

seal off an entrance. At the foot of the slab, in a rudimentary sepulchre, lay the skeletons of probably six young people of whom at least one was female. . . . The foreheads were artificially deformed and traces of incrustations in the teeth suggest that they were nobles and not slaves. There was no offering accom-

94

panying these remains, but the fact that they were at the entrance to a sealed chamber pointed to something of singular importance. On June 15, 1952, we were able to make the stone turn and we entered the mysterious chamber we had been so eagerly seeking since 1949.

The crossing of the threshold was, of course, a moment of indescribable emotion. I was in a spacious crypt that seemed to be carved in ice since its walls were covered with a shiny calcareous layer and numerous stalactites hung from the vault like curtains and thick stalagmites gave the impression of huge candles. . . .

The most surprising aspect of the crypt is unquestionably the huge monument that takes up most of the space. The first thing seen was a horizontal stone slab . . . the sides and upper face of which was carved. The slab was resting on a monolithic block . . . the sides of which were also carved. Lastly, the

entire group was held up by six monolithic supports 4 of which were carved. This monument weighed approximately 20 tons. Evidently the crypt and inner stairway joining it to the temple had been built precisely to hide this monument. . . .

[The] moment when I found that the supposed substructure of the hypothetical altar was hollow moved me almost as strongly as the discovery of the crypt itself. . . . Thus the lifting of the slab was now indispensable no matter what the difficulties and risks. Using truck jacks set on tree trunks under the corners of the slab we were able to lift it. The operation of bringing the tree trunks into the crypt, placing them properly and the delicate task of raising the slab lasted from 6 a.m. November 27, 1952 to the same hour on the 28th. That is to say, I spent 24 consecutive hours without leaving the crypt.

As the slab was raised, a peculiar cavity carved out of the enormous block upon which it rested could be discerned. . . . It was sealed by a highly polished perfectly fitting stone cover with 4 perforations closed by stone plugs. As soon as the space allowed, I slipped under the slab, removed two of the plugs and shone my flashlight through one of them, and looking through the other—a few centimeters from my eyes—was a human skull covered with pieces of jade.

Slipping some ropes through the holes we lifted off the lid in a way similar to that used by the priests to set it in place. The funerary receptacle came into view with its spectacular contents surrounded by the vivid vermillion of the cinnabar with which the walls and the bottom of the cavity of the coffin were covered. . . .

96

The brilliant green of the jade stood out sharply against the red background of the cinnabar-covered coffin and bones. The personage had been buried with all his jade jewels: he held a beautiful bead like a coin in his mouth to exchange for food in the other world. On his forehead, he had a diadem made of small discs from which [hung] a little plaque in the form of the bat god; his hair was separated into locks by little tubes. Earplugs made up of several pieces lay on either side of his head.

Various rows of beads were around his neck, and over his ribs a broad pectoral of tubular beads. From each arm, we recovered a bracelet of 200 small beads and a thick jade ring from each finger of both hands. The right hand held a thick cubic bead and the left a spherical one. There were more beads near his feet as well as a splendid jade figurine probably representing the sun god. (Alberto Ruz, *The Civilization of the Ancient Maya*, pp. 110–116.)

At Bonampak the structures are set around a rectangular plaza. The most important is the Temple of Paintings, so named because it contains a series of fresco paintings which cover the walls from floor to ceiling. The paintings, originally in brilliant tones of blue, red, brown, yellow, green, orange, and white, show scenes of religious processionals, warfare, and political negotiation. Evidence such as this has demonstrated that a strong religious component to a culture does not necessarily imply pacifism; the religious leaders of the major ceremonial centers were probably leaders in war as well and were therefore assuming political responsibilities for their communities.

Murals from Room 1 of the Temple of Paintings at Bonampak. These show a ceremonial scene. The four figures in the center, on the east wall, are part of a procession which continues to the south. Their white capes were probably made of cotton, and their headdresses were of feathers and animal skins.

Mural from Room 2 of the Temple of Paintings. Here warriors engaged in a battle use spears, carry shields, and brandish clubs. Some wear headdresses of jaguar skins, others wear quetzal feathers. Toward the right a conqueror grasps a fallen enemy by the hair. The glyphs in the background of these murals explain what is taking place.

All these sites are in the central and southern parts of the Maya Lowland region. Outstanding in the northern region is Uxmal in Yucatán, the largest site in the Puuc style. This style is characterized by the use on façades of high-relief stone mosaics which create patterns of bright light and deep shade. It inspired the construction of a similar façade at the National Museum of Anthropology in Mexico City. Four major constructions at Uxmal have been excavated: two temple pyramids, called the Temple of the Dwarf and the Temple of the Magician, and two multiroomed structures called the Nunnery and the Governor's Palace. The architectural style of the Puuc sites, and especially of Uxmal, has been considered more imaginative and sophisticated both in concept and execution than that of the sites in the other Mayan regions.

The Nunnery and the Temple of the Magician at Uxmal in Yucatán. The Nunnery (*left*), so named by the Spaniards, consists of four long buildings which form a quadrangle. The Temple of the Magician (*right*) is more than 30 meters high. These buildings show an impressive contrast in the use of space.

Chichén Itzá, perhaps the best-known site in Yucatán, is not far from Uxmal and was also built in the Puuc style. Among the buildings exhibiting this style are the Nunnery, the Church, and the long building called Akab Dzib ("obscure writing") because of the sculptured hieroglyphs on one of its lintels. The heyday of Chichén Itzá came several hundred years later.

West building of the Nunnery, Uxmal. More than 50 meters long, it has
seven small rooms which open out into a spacious quadrangle reached
by a broad stairway. The vertical frieze on top of the building shows
masks, small huts, and thrones. Over the central doorway is a throne
with a standing figure, half-man, half-turtle, under a feathered canopy.

INTERDEPENDENCE OF DIVERSE REGIONS

WHAT is seen in Mesoamerica between A.D. 250 and 600
is not only the flowering of two patterns of complex society, as exemplified on the one hand by Teotihuacan in the
Valley of Mexico and Monte Albán in the Valley of
Oaxaca, and on the other by the great centers in the Maya
lowland region, but also a close interdependence of the
different environmental and cultural regions. The archaeological evidence for this consists of ceramic vessels char-

101

acteristic of a particular region but found in other regions, and natural products from one source which were used far from it.

While there is a great deal of evidence of local interchanges within zones and between adjacent zones, the pattern which characterizes this period is that of Teotihuacan dominance over the entire area. Teotihuacan artifacts and artifact characteristics, as well as natural products from the Valley of Mexico, are found at innumerable places throughout Mesoamerica, from western Mexico to the Maya highlands.

A number of archaeologists have seen trade as the mechanism which accounts for the distribution of these artifacts and products. Was it open and free trade in which craftsmen and producers dealt directly with consumers? Two factors militate against such an interpretation. First, the distances involved were sometimes thousands of kilometers, which had to be traversed without pack animals or wheeled carts; the transport of goods then, required full-time traders. Second, study of the settlement and zone patterns at Teotihuacan and in the Valley of Mexico has shown that Teotihuacan society was well organized and highly integrated, with a large and effective bureaucracy. Trade, since it involved many segments of that society, could only have been possible if it were carried out under the direction of the rulers and their subordinates. Teotihuacan's trade throughout Mesoamerica would appear to have been in the hands of full-time specialists who, if they were not precisely civil servants, were guided by the bureaucracy of Teotihuacan and responsible to it.

Some archaeologists have interpreted the data as indicating that the trading network was based on tribute or that there was some colonization, but there is no good evidence that trade carried with it political controls in the sense that the trading territory was a political empire. It appears to have been integrated only economically into Teotihuacan society.

At Teotihuacan the inter-regional symbiotic relationship which had been established by the Olmec was regulated and intensified under the control of a group whose existence was an outgrowth of urban society. It established an economic relationship between settlement and territory which had never before existed in Mesoamerica. The transformation of the economic relationship into a political one was the next major development in the course of culture change in Mesoamerica.

Sometime around A.D. 650 the great centers of the highlands and the lowlands began to fall. Teotihuacan was burned in 700; Monte Albán was abandoned by 1000. Copán stopped functioning soon after 800, and one by one the other Lowland Maya ceremonial centers were deserted. By 900 calendrical dates had ceased to be recorded on commemorative stelae. There have been many historical explanations for the collapse of these centers, such as invasion, disease, crop failure, or combinations of these. But from the point of view of cultural change, the question is why the societies were incapable of withstanding or combatting these events. Perhaps elaboration of the established patterns had reached its culmination. The societies had reached the limits of growth possible within the confines of the old pattern. The new stresses demanded new cultural configurations. The molds were broken, and fresh ones, fashioned from the clay of the old, were made.

7

THE TOLTECS: POLITICAL
INNOVATORS

THE date A.D. 900 is of major importance in Mesoamerican prehistory because it marks the rise of the city of
Tula, the capital of the Toltecs. The site lies outside the
Valley of Mexico in the state of Hidalgo but in the same
kind of semi-arid highland environmental zone. Its loca-
tion is different from those of Teotihuacan or Monte
Albán in that it stands for the most part on a long irregular
north-south ridge overlooking the valley, rather than in
the valley itself. The position was militarily strategic for
both offensive and defensive action in relation to the site
and the cultivable lands in the valley.

THE TOLTECS: POLITICAL INNOVATORS

EXPLORATIONS AT TULA

PRESENT knowledge of the site is due largely to the work of Jorge Acosta, who conducted excavations there between 1940 and 1955. Further investigations have been carried on by Eduardo Matos of the Mexican National Institute of Anthropology and History and by Richard A. Diehl of the University of Missouri. Diehl has been concerned particularly with determining the settlement pattern of the site and interpreting the organization of Toltec society.

Diehl's investigations have revealed that Tula at its maximum size covered at least 8.3 square kilometers, and he estimates that further work will reveal its size to have been at least 10 or 11 square kilometers. The surface was covered with artifacts and other cultural remains, from which Diehl infers a large, dense resident population, although probably a smaller one than that of Teotihuacan. He has uncovered a number of multi-storied habitations and believes that possibly these, instead of the single-story *barrios* found at Teotihuacan, were the basic housing units. He has also located some workshops and suggests that miners, knappers making obsidian and flint tools, ceramicists, construction workers, stone carvers, carpenters, and lapidaries practiced their crafts in the city. While there were also agricultural specialists such as cultivators of cotton, nopal (a kind of cactus), and maguey, and processors of maguey, the majority of the population may have been artisans rather than farmers.

The ceremonial and civic activities of the city were conducted on a number of small hills. The major one, however, is the one which has been excavated and has constituted what has been known up to now as Tula. Clustered

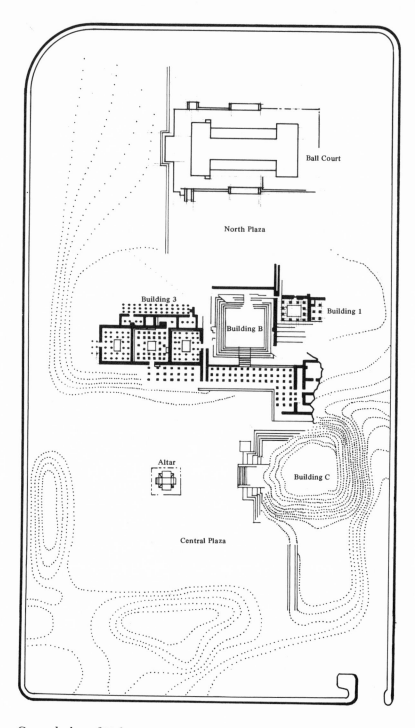

Ground plan of Tula

in the main area around a plaza are five major constructions, Building B, Building 1, Building C, Building 3, and a ball court.

Building B is a pyramidal structure with five levels and a wide stairway on one side. It is 40 meters square at its base and 10 meters high. The vertical panels which constituted each level were apparently faced with carved slabs. Although the facing has for the most part been lost, some of the slabs have been recovered and show motifs of eagles and vultures devouring bleeding hearts, alternating with human faces emerging from the fangs of plumed serpents. Above the panels is a frieze of treading felines.

Building B at Tula. One of several major constructions on a central plaza, this is a pyramidal platform with a colonnaded gallery at the front and side. The figures on the summit originally supported the roof of the superstructure.

Sculptured warrior figures on Building B, Tula. These statues, in battle dress with dart throwers in their right hands, are among many motifs at Tula testifying to the Toltecs' militarism.

On the summit of the pyramid were four statues of warriors nearly 5 meters high and carved square columns of the same height also showing warrior figures. The warriors are all elaborately costumed. Each wears a feathered headdress, ear-pieces, a butterfly-shaped breastplate,

108

bead necklace, clasped belt, embroidered breechclout, and bracelets, anklets, and sandals. Each carries darts and a dart thrower, a "sword" (a curved stick into which obsidian blades may have been inserted), and a knife tucked into the bracelet on the upper left arm. Each figure also carries a small gourd which may have contained copal, a resin used perhaps in ceremonies connected with battle.

In front of the stairway of the great pyramid stood a columned vestibule 55 meters long and 15 meters wide. Behind the pyramid is the remains of what has been called the Serpent Wall. It consists of a central frieze framed above and below by friezes of carved, painted meanders. The central frieze has a repetitive motif of a corpse being eaten by a serpent. The skull is seen between the serpent's fangs, and the arms and legs are intertwined with its body.

Building 1 is immediately to the east of Building B and built against it. In the center of this structure was a shallow sunken patio surrounded by twelve square columns that probably held up the roof. Many rooms opened out onto the patio. It has been suggested that these rooms were the apartments of the priests who serviced the adjoining temple, but Acosta believes that they were reception rooms dedicated to the gods honored at the temple.

Building C is another stepped, stairwayed pyramid, even larger than Building B. The superstructure is gone, but near the pyramid were found two statues of life-sized reclining figures called Chacmool, each facing to the side with a receptacle on the stomach, and these are believed to have constituted part of the superstructure.

Building 3 lies to the west of Building B. It was probably surrounded on three sides by columns. Three large halls and five small rooms have been excavated. Acosta believes that Building 3 was a palace used for civil affairs rather than religious ceremonies, since religious rituals usually took place at the top of pyramids. Some of the small rooms may have been used for civil events or government business; others may have been the apartments of members of the political bureaucracy, perhaps even of the ruler of Tula. There is a ball court in this area, an elongated patio, 67 by 12.5 meters, with lateral extensions at both ends. It is below ground level and is flanked by walls resting on low platforms. Apertures on the walls formerly held the rings through which the rubber ball passed during the game. Found in association with the ball court were several pieces of sculpture, among them a ball player with gloves, knee-guards, and a thick belt.

Tula appears to have been an urban settlement with its large population differentiated on a number of social and economic levels, and with a nucleus in which civil and religious events on behalf of the community took place. It seems to have been cut from the same pattern as Teotihuacan, albeit on a smaller scale. It was, however, different from Teotihuacan in one significant way: its military system appears more specialized. The changing shape of the military system is seen in Tula's defensive position, in the warrior sculptures, and in the concern with defeat and death depicted in the friezes.

SPREAD OF TOLTEC INFLUENCE

THE new military configuration seems to be the herald of a shift or reorganization of society in which innovations in the military system made for changes in the political system. A strong military establishment makes possible and enforces the political goals of the community. In every great Mesoamerican center the survival of the political community depended upon its successful exploitation of the area. The pattern of economic exchange created by the Olmec was expanded and improved by the Teotihuacanos. In Toltec times the trade pattern which most benefited the community of Tula seems to have been established through force of arms. The traders, while free agents, were incorporated into the military-political system. Their places of trade were probably designated by the political bureaucracy and they were given the necessary force to establish and maintain their economic relationships.

It is fortunate that for this period information is available not only in archaeological evidence but also from the legendary histories written down after the Spanish conquest. The archaeological data from Tula itself show, on the basis of ceramic analysis, what appears to be trade contact with Nicaragua, Costa Rica, and the Gulf coast. Copper may show contact with Michoacán. Marine shells found at Tula have been identified as coming both from the Gulf of Mexico and from the Pacific coast.

The distribution of Toltec artifacts and cultural traits is particularly extensive in the north and west. The important sites in the north are the Schroeder site in Durango and those at Chalchihuites and La Quemada; those in the west are Ixtlán del Rio in Nayarit and Cojumatlán, Zacapu, Tzintzuntzan, and Apatzingán in Michoacán. To the east in the Huasteca region (which includes the coast and interior of northern Veracruz and southern Tamaulipas as well as San Luis Potosí and part of Hidalgo), the sites of Las Flores and Tamuín show Toltec influence. Toltec cultural traits are found to the south in the Valley of Mexico and beyond in Xochicalco and Teloloapan and perhaps extended to Tututepec in coastal Oaxaca. In the Mayan area the site which shows the most spectacular Toltec influence is Chichén Itzá in the northern lowlands, which existed in earlier times but achieved its importance after A.D. 600.

The documentary sources interpreted by the Mexican ethnohistorian Wigberto Jiménez Moreno tell something about the relationship between Tula and the contemporary settlements throughout Mesoamerica. About twenty settlements, mostly to the east and south, were part of an entity called "the Great Tollan"—the old name for Tula. Other places are named as having been conquered by rulers of Tula and some centers are said to have shared power with Tula.

What is not suggested by either archaeological or documentary evidence is much centralization of political power in the hands of the bureaucracy at Tula. The archaeological data reveal strong local styles with some Toltec traits, never Toltec domination. The documents, in noting that Tula "shared power" with other centers, indicate that Tula was by no means in control of political power within its own trading territory.

The evidence suggests that Tula achieved political influence over its trade network by means of its military system. The military arm established and enforced trade relations, and since trade was controlled by the political bureaucracy, the communities in the network were drawn into a loose political arrangement. But local autonomy was never lost, and the communities were not integrated into the Tula political system.

Some connections seem to have been unrelated to the economic and political network. The Toltec influence at

THE TOLTECS: POLITICAL INNOVATORS

Chichén Itzá appears to have a largely stylistic significance. Sometime after the initial construction, a new section was added. Among the new constructions were the Temple of the Warriors, the Group of a Thousand Columns, the Castillo, the Skull Rack, the Temple of Chacmool, and a great ball court. The small narrow rooms of the earlier temples were replaced by an open interior and grand colonnades. The feathered serpent, warrior processions, stalking felines, eagles, and scenes of sacrificial victims became common motifs in sculpture and carvings. The Mayan gods made room for deities such as Quetzalcoatl, the feathered serpent god; Texcatlipoca, the sky god; Tlalchitonatiuh, the god of the warrior cult; Chicomecoatl, the maize goddess; and Tlaloc, the rain god. Warrior figures were depicted in sculpture. While some of these architectural and iconographic changes developed out of the local style, others are considered Toltec.

Despite the infusion of Toltec traits, Chichén Itzá remained Maya in character. As Muriel Weaver of Hunter College noted in *The Aztecs, Maya and Their Predecessors*, "The innovations were Toltec, but the execution was Maya, and the basic techniques remained unchanged." Legendary history records that a group of Toltecs came to Chichén Itzá and achieved power. They were, however, not agents of Tula sent out to carve an empire, but outcasts whose economic and political connections with their mother city had been severed completely. Although the wave of Toltec culture undoubtedly originated in Tula there is no reason to believe that the Mayan center was governed by the Toltec bureaucracy.

The Castillo at Chichén Itzá, seen from the top of the Temple of the Warriors. In the foreground at right is the Chacmool, a reclining figure with a basin in its stomach; at left is the base of a feathered serpent column, formed by the open jaws of the serpent. The Castillo, one of the later constructions at Chichén Itzá, stands in an immense clearing where thousands of people could gather to participate in the rites held in the small stone temple on top of the quadrilateral base pyramid.

OUTSIDE THE TOLTEC SPHERE

IT should be remembered that by no means all of Mesoamerica was part of the Toltec network or even periph-
erally connected as was Chichén Itzá. Some settlements
and zones remained totally outside the Toltec sphere of
influence. Two important settlements of this kind were
Mitla in Oaxaca and Cholula in the state of Puebla.

Ceramic sherds found at Mitla, which lies at the east

end of the Valley of Oaxaca, show that the site was occupied in earlier times but all its structures date from the period after the fall of Monte Albán. The ruins that have been excavated have been found clustered in five groups around the Mitla River and its small tributaries. Three of these—the Group of Columns, the Arroyo Group, and the Curacy or Church Group—are alike in consisting of apartments surrounding a rectangular patio. The other two, the South Group and the Adobe Group, have not been as completely excavated but appear to be characterized by pyramidal structures. Tombs have been found under two of the pyramids in the South Group.

The buildings had the usual Mesoamerican rubble core and were faced with stone covered with plaster or trachite. The façades are made of mosaics of stone which form geometric motifs worked into various patterns. In some cases, such as in the Group of Columns, an imitation of mosaic was created by carving the motifs into a single large stone.

An analysis of the stratigraphy and artifacts associated with the South Group by Ignacio Bernal, a well-known Mexican archaeologist, shows it to have been occupied during the heyday of Monte Albán by the same people who lived there, the Zapotecs. After the fall of Monte Albán the Zapotecs continued to occupy Mitla and were later joined there by a group called the Mixtecs, which was emerging as a cultural entity at this time. Mitla was a mixture of the older Zapotec and the newer Mixtec culture. This conclusion is based on the architectural style, which, according to Bernal, combines Zapotec elements with new features, such as the "elaborate decoration of stone mosaic, the use of enormous monoliths, and the general arrangement of rooms," which he believes are

116

Typical mosaic façade of a building at Mitla.

Mixtec. (*The Mixtecs in the Archaeology of the Valley of Oaxaca,* p. 346.)

Not enough is known about the settlement pattern at Mitla to talk about the nature of the society. It is possible that there was a fortification, in which case Mitla may have been, like the later Mixtec fortified centers, warring for control of an economic and political territory.

Cholula too was occupied earlier and was under the influence of Teotihuacan. Even after that city fell, Teotihua-

117

Polychrome Mixteca-Puebla bowl found in a tomb at Zaachila in Oaxaca, National Museum of Anthropology, Mexico City. This bowl, about 15 centimeters high, has a warm orange slip and is painted in green, red, brown, black, and white. The hummingbird on the lip is a brilliant blue.

can culture persisted at Cholula. Around A.D. 800 Cholula was conquered by a group of people called the Olmeca-Xicalanca (who were in no way related to the earlier Olmec of southern Veracruz and Tabasco). As with Mitla, there is not enough information about the settlement pattern of Cholula to draw inferences about economic, social, and political life. But the distribution of its distinctive ceramic ware suggests that Cholula, an important Mixteca-Puebla center, may have had strong economic ties with sites to the north in the present state of Tlaxcala and to the south in Puebla.

Gold jewelry made by Mixtec craftsmen, American Museum of Natural History, New York. The pair of ear plugs (*top*) were inserted through holes in the ear lobes; the lip plug (*below left*) was pushed through a slit in the lower lip. Small dangling bells embellish the ear plugs as well as the ring (*below right*). The Mixtecs were highly skilled in metalwork, an art which was not fully established until after A.D. 900.

THE TOLTECS: POLITICAL INNOVATORS

THE PASSING OF THE TOLTECS

SOMETIME before A.D. 1200 Tula fell. There is archaeological evidence of a fire sweeping through the center. Legendary history attributes the destruction to invaders from the north. Certainly the fact that Tula was never rebuilt indicates that its annihilation was not merely an accident, but a military-political event.

Pedro Armillas, an archaeologist who has lived in Mexico and in the United States, has sought explanations of the causes of the invasion. He suggests that in the first millennium of the Christian era the agricultural boundary was moving northward, until, around A.D. 1000, it reached the geographical limits, between the 22nd and 23rd parallels, beyond which the environment, with existing technology, was unsuited to the cultivation of crops. The limit of complex society lay between the 20th and 21st parallels just north of Tula. The zone between these two sets of parallels is seen by Armillas as a "cultural gradient." Within it lay habitation sites of varying size, some with a fairly large, dense population and public structures. A number of the larger sites were fortified, suggesting military and political relationships with their neighbors. North of this zone, to judge from the settlements, were seminomadic peoples, who depended largely on a hunting and gathering economy although they may have engaged in some marginal farming. To the south were the complex societies based on more secure methods of food production. The cultural gradient zone was a buffer between the seminomads of the north and the fully settled populations to the south.

Perhaps a climatic change occurred, which may not have been severe, but was sufficient to shift ecological

119

relationships in the buffer zone. In any case, archaeo-logical evidence of the abandonment of sites and the leg-endary histories show that some time around the end of the twelfth century A.D the farmers of the buffer zone, ap-parently no longer able to wrest a living from their land, moved down *en masse* into the verdant region south of the 20th parallel. Armillas estimates that the area of the buffer zone amounted to about 60,000 square kilometers, and the information from settlement studies suggests that very large numbers of people were involved in the migra-tion.

But even more important, the seminomads of the north, who were called the Chichimecs, no longer contained by the buffer zone, came swooping down into Mesoamerica. The Toltec community, its numbers increased by mass migration and its food supply reduced by poor harvests (possibly as a result of the same climatic change), could not withstand this invasion. Ultimately Tula was burned, and the Toltecs moved out into the Valley of Mexico, the Valley of Puebla, and as far south as Guatemala, to be-come integrated with other groups and to form small po-litical entities lending their prestigious name and cultural heritage to the newly established communities.

8

THE AZTECS: WARRIORS IN SEARCH OF AN EMPIRE

THE Chichimecs who destroyed the Toltec regime were also the founders of a new society. A group of immigrant Chichimecs serving in the Toltec army, who were called Aztecs after their mythical home Aztlan, built the great city of Tenochtitlán and established by means of their military system a territory based on economic ties which gradually developed a new kind of political conformation.

The Aztecs seem to have wandered around Meso-america for a number of years. Their first settlement appears to have been at Chapultepec, where they lived for perhaps twenty-five or fifty years. Sometime between A.D.

121

1299 and 1323, they were defeated by their neighbors in the Valley of Mexico and forced to leave. More years of wandering ensued, but in about 1345 they founded what was to become the city of Tenochtitlán.

This most important center is described in historical records, but unfortunately very little archaeological investigation of it has been possible. When the Spaniards laid siege to the city, they found their advance hindered by deep ditches crossing the streets. They therefore demolished the houses and used the rubble to fill in the ditches so that their horses and artillery pieces could move unimpeded. After their victory, finding that stone was scarce, they tore down Aztec monuments and buildings in order to get the material to build Mexico City. The knowledge that it was politically and religiously expedient to rid the city of all vestiges of the former society probably added to their zeal. What was left of Tenochtitlán, which had been built on an island in the middle of Lake Texcoco, began sinking slowly into the mud. The combination of natural forces, the destruction of the old structures, and the building of new ones over their remains has left very little of the Aztec capital accessible to the shovels of archaeologists.

Most of our knowledge of Tenochtitlán is based on descriptions written in the sixteenth and seventeenth centuries. The city was connected to the mainland by three major causeways: the northern causeway led to Tepeyacac, the western to Tlacopan, and the southern, which had two branches, to Iztapalapa and to Coyoacán. The causeways continued to the heart of the city and seem to have been its main highways of traffic. Bernal Díaz del Castillo, one of the Spanish conquerors, described the crowds on the southern causeway when the Spaniards entered the city:

> Early the next day we left Iztapalapa with a large escort . . . we proceeded along the Causeway which is here eight paces in width and runs so straight to [Tenochtitlán] that it does not seem to me to turn either much or little, but broad as it is, it was so crowded with people that there was hardly room for them all, some of them going to and others returning from [Tenochtitlán], besides those who had come out to see us, so that we were hardly able to pass by the crowds of them that came; and the towers and [temples] were full of people as well as the canoes from all parts of the lake. (*The Discovery and Conquest of Mexico,* pp. 191–192.)

Within the city, in addition to the causeways, there were three types of arteries: canals, roads, and roads bordered by canals. Where the canals cut across the roads, the Aztecs built bridges with huge wooden beams. Hernán Cortés, the captain of the Spanish conquerors, described these thoroughfares in a letter to his king:

> The city is as large as Seville or Cordova; its streets, I speak of the principal ones, are very wide and straight; some of these and all the inferior ones, are half land and half water, and are navigated by canoes. All the streets at intervals have openings, through which water flows, crossing one street to another; and at these openings, some of which are very wide, there are pieces of timber, of great strength and well put together; on many of these bridges ten

horses can be abreast. (*The Despatches of Hernándo Cortés*, pp. 111–112.)

The area of the city, including an island called Tlatelolco which became part of the greater Tenochtitlán community and small islands on the lake used for agriculture, is estimated at approximately 7.5 square kilometers. The city was built around a nuclear area of temples and public buildings. The most important of these was the great quadrangle of the Templo Mayor, which was approximately 500 meters square and included, be-

Reconstruction of Tenochtitlán. This city, the capital of the Aztecs and the key to the Spaniards' conquest of Mexico, was largely destroyed by zealous missionaries and practical builders, but much of it remains under present-day Mexico City. Excavations for subway tunnels and power lines still reveal the remnants of temples such as these.

sides the Templo Mayor itself, about seventy-five other structures, among them smaller temples, ball courts, skull altars, houses of priests and youths training for the priesthood, arsenals, and workshops.

Although Cortés abhorred and reviled the Aztec religion, he admired the grand architectural conception of the Templo Mayor and described it with the appreciation of a sightseer viewing a classic European monument:

Among these temples there is one which far surpasses all the rest, whose grandeur of architectural details no human tongue is able to describe; for within its precincts surrounded by a lofty wall, there is room enough for a town of five hundred families. Around the interior of this enclosure there are handsome edifices, containing large halls and corridors, in which the religious persons attached to the temple reside. There are full forty towers, which are lofty and well-built, the largest of which has fifty steps leading to its main body, and is higher than the tower of the principal church at Seville. The stone and wood of which they are constructed are so well wrought in every part, that nothing could be better done, for the interior of the chapels containing the idols consists of curious imagery, wrought in stone, with plaster ceilings, and wood-work carved in relief, and painted with figures of monsters and other objects. . . . There are three halls in this grand temple, which contain the principal idols, these are of wonderful extent and height, and admirable workmanship, adorned with figures sculptured in stone and wood; leading from the halls are chapels with very small doors, to which the light is not admitted,

125

nor are any persons except the priests, and not all of them. (*Cortés*, pp. 115–116.)

The city was divided into four major units. Each of these contained separate residential wards, the numbers of which have been estimated as ranging from twenty to seventy. While population estimates for Tenochtitlán have been as low as 60,000 and as high as 300,000, the most reliable appears to be between 60,000 and 120,000. The lower-class residential complexes consisted of a number of small separate buildings—a kitchen, storage bin, sweatbath, and bedrooms—surrounding a central patio. The construction was simple: stone and adobe walls with a thatched roof. The houses of the upper classes had the same ground plan, but there were splendid apartments off the center patio, sometimes rising two stories. Cortés wrote:

> There was one palace somewhat inferior to the rest, attached to which was a beautiful garden with balconies extending over it, supported by marble columns, and having a floor formed of jasper elegantly inlaid. There were apartments in this palace sufficient to lodge two princes of the highest rank with their retinues. There were likewise belonging to it ten pools of water, in which were kept the different species of water birds found in this country. . . . The water is let off at certain times to keep it pure, and is replenished by means of pipes. (*Cortés,* pp. 121–122.)

Sanders has suggested on the basis of both archaeological and ethnohistorical data that the majority of the population of Tenochtitlán were not food producers, but

126

craftsmen, educated and maintained by guilds. Their products were sold in the two great daily markets in the city and traded far into the hinterlands by another important group of specialists, the *pochteca*, or long-distance traders. In addition there were the priests and the members of the military-political bureaucracy. Besides occupational specialization, there were different degrees of access to economic resources. Occupational and economic factors were closely interrelated with social stratification. There were two main social strata: nobility and commoners. The nobility consisted of those individuals who held political office, controlled land, and received tribute. The commoners were ruled, worked land or produced craft goods, and paid tribute in the form of labor and products.

One activity seems to have cut across class lines. Warriors were numbered among the nobles as well as the commoners, and indeed success in warfare provided a means of moving from the commoner to the noble class. Young male commoners entered "houses of youth" where they were trained in skills such as brick making, house building, grave digging, and cultivation of the soil, and also in the art of warfare. As part of their training they were taken into battle under the supervision of experienced warriors and afterward were considered part of the reserve to be called up at time of war. Moderate success in battle was rewarded by advancement to the position of leader among commoner youths. Greater success meant that the commoner was given the title of *Tequihua*, received privileges of certain dress, was permitted to take part in the war council, and qualified for government jobs. Some of these warriors moved on to serve on the ruler's war council or became the ruler's administrators. Others may have achieved still higher administrative and judiciary posts, but most of the documentary reports record that the highest offices were filled only by nobles. Exceptionally courageous deeds in war could elevate commoners into the group called the Brown Knights, and they then became members of the noble class. As nobles they were exempted from tribute payments, were given their own land, and their titles and possessions were inheritable.

The sons of noble families who dedicated themselves to war belonged to a variety of ranked military societies and served in special military positions both on and off the battlefield. The war council, which was made up of nobles, was responsible for strategy. It decided on the best means of attack from information obtained by spies who were usually long-distance traders. A map was drawn, the roads leading to the enemy town were marked, and the points of entry agreed upon. This done, the council would send out the order for all able-bodied men to assemble. In battle the nobles formed the vanguard of the army or commanded small groups, and the bravest served as the rearguard, while the commoners marched and fought in units based on kinship.

Tenochtitlán, then, had an urban society similar to those of Teotihuacan and Tula. The settlement was a city with a nuclear center of public buildings and a habitation area occupied by a large, dense population differentiated on the basis of wealth, occupation, and control of political power. Tula and Tenochtitlán, however, differed from Teotihuacan in two critical ways: their farming populations lived outside the city limits for the most part, and their military systems were far more specialized. These two characteristics were both more pronounced in Tenochtitlán than in Tula, and they shaped Tenochtitlán's relationship to its zone and territory.

The necessity of relying on the rural population to provide food for the city fostered a close relationship between the city and the rural area. Studies of the settlement pattern by William Sanders and Jeffrey Parsons have shown that in the Valley of Mexico during the Aztec period there were sixty communities, each with a population of at least 12,000 and in some cases as many as 50,000, each covering an area of approximately 130 square kilometers, and each consisting of an administrative center and small dependent hamlets and villages. These communities paid tribute either to Tenochtitlán or to one of the other two great centers, Tlacopan and Texcoco. Those attached to Tenochtitlán appear to have been well integrated into the political system controlled by the bureaucracy of Tenochtitlán, and city and rural settlements formed a single community. The political power of Tenochtitlán, then, extended beyond the city into the zone. What had been an economic relationship in Teotihuacan times became a political one with the Aztecs.

The military system was the device which permitted the politicizing of economic relations in the territory. The Aztecs had the personnel, matériel, strategy, and tactics to launch the series of wars which they carried on for nearly two hundred years and which brought into the Aztec trade network, more than four hundred towns, from Hidalgo in the north to the borders of Guatemala in the south. Once caught in the network as a result of defeat in battle, a community could not escape without fighting and winning another war. There are indications that the communities in the Aztec territory were not as loosely connected as those in the Toltec territory had been. For one

129

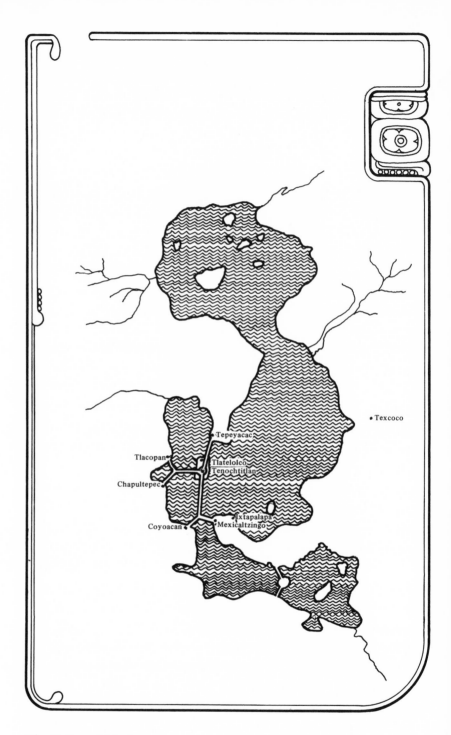

The Valley of Mexico

thing, the military-political bureaucracy at Tenochtitlán seems to have been in closer control. Just before the conquest, the *pochteca*, formerly an important although subordinate part of the military-political system, were being systemically moved out of the system and replaced by bureaucrats. First they were excluded from the military societies, then they were persecuted, and finally they were eliminated by death sentences. While the ostensible reasons for this course of action are hard to determine, the effect was to shift power from the traders to the members of the military-political system. The bureaucracy began to send out selected members to live in outlying settlements as representatives of Tenochtitlán. The lines of connection between Tenochtitlán and the communities of the territory were pulled tighter by the presence of officials who, unlike the traders, were carrying out political directives on behalf of the mother city.

Yet there was no great centralization of power. Most communities had no resident officials and maintained their political autonomy. Even those that had such officials were only partly affected, since political marriages between officials and the local nobility tended to keep community interests in the foreground.

While the Aztecs held the most extensive territory in Mesoamerica, they were by no means the exclusive power. There were a number of independent territories that were equally complex and perhaps were on the road to even greater military specialization and centralization of political control. The two most important were those of the Tarascans and the Tlaxcalans. The Tarascans were immediately to the west in what is now Michoacán, and the Tlaxcalans shared the Aztecs' eastern border. The Aztecs fought many wars with both but never defeated

131

either. They made no successful incursions into Tarascan or Tlaxcalan territories, and the two held fast to their power.

Perhaps the Tarascan and Tlaxcalan societies represent what would have been the next configuration of Meso-american society, had the conquest not intervened. In that pattern the military system aided the formation of an in-tegrated territory in which all political control was firmly in the hands of the major center. If that change had oc-curred, it too would have sprung from seeds sown by the Olmec. For despite the differences in environmental zones and the varieties of societal organization, all com-plex Mesoamerican cultures were marked by differentia-tion among men on the basis of wealth, political power, and occupation, and by integration of many kinds of com-munities into a functioning unit.

AFTERWORD

In 1519 the Spaniards landed in Mexico, and within the next few years they had wrested power from all the great centers. They reorganized society in their own image, changing the path of the indigenous development. Yet native culture was not snuffed out. The marvelous intellectual achievements were destroyed and the men who had the knowledge to create them were killed or eventually simply died. But something remained. It was a whisper of the huge, booming voice of Indian culture. Archaeologists became the custodians of that faint, indistinct, remnant sound. They tried to hear it, to understand it, and to interpret it. They took on the responsibility of presenting not only a facsimile of the original but also an explanation of how these societies came into being, why they took one form rather than another, and what made them change.

It is this mission that sends them on reconnaissances to find sites, directs their excavations, and guides their laboratory work. Material remains—ceramics, stones, pollen, animal bones—of which a single season's investigation can yield several hundred thousand, are meaningful only as they contribute to the accomplishment of the mission. Relating those to the whole is what archaeology is about, and the results of archaeological work have revealed the prehistory of Mexico.

Conversion Table

Chronological Table

Glossary

Selected Bibliography

Index

CONVERSION TABLE

Weight
1 kilogram = 2.20 pounds

Length
1 centimeter = 0.39 inch
1 meter = 39.37 inches
1 kilometer = 0.62 mile

Area
1 square kilometer = 0.39 square mile

CHRONOLOGICAL TABLE

	PERIOD	CULTURE	
20,000– 7000 B.C.	Paleo-American		
7000– 2000/ 1500 B.C.	Food-Collecting and Incipient Cultivation		
1500 B.C.– A.D. 250	Preclassic	Olmec	1250– 400 B.C.
A.D. 250– 900	Classic	Maya Teotihuacan Monte Albán	A.D. 300– 800 A.D. 1–700 600 B.C.– A.D. 1000
A.D. 900– 1519/1521	Postclassic	Toltec Aztec	A.D. 900– 1187 A.D. 1345– 1519/1521

GLOSSARY

ADZ—a stone tool with a cutting edge hafted at right angles to the handle.

ARTIFACT—an object manufactured by man; any material result of human behavior.

AWL—a pointed object used for piercing small holes, especially in leather.

AX—a stone tool with a sharp cutting edge hafted with the edge parallel to the longitudinal axis of the handle.

BARRIO (Spanish)—a residential quarter.

BLADE—a stone flake, at least twice as long as it is wide, with parallel sides.

CELT—an ungrooved ax.

CHIPPED STONE—objects made by percussion and/or pressure flaking.

CHOPPER—a tool with one flaked edge, used for cutting.

EAR PLUG—an ornamental object worn in a hole in the lobe of the ear.

GRAVER—a small tool with a sharp point, used in marking and slitting bone, wood, and antler.

GROUND STONE—objects manufactured by pecking and/or abrading.

INTER-REGIONAL SYMBIOTIC NETWORK—term used by William Sanders for mutual trading units of differing climates and productions.

LIP PLUG—an ornamental object worn in a hole in the lower lip.

MANO—a handstone used in conjunction with a metate for grinding maize.

METATE—a shallow trough-shaped stone used in conjunction with a mano for grinding maize.

MILPA—a plot of cultivated land.

MORTAR—a deep, comparatively narrow basin used in conjunction with a pestle for pulverizing foodstuffs.

MULLER—an egg-shaped stone used in pulverizing.

NUCLEATED CENTER—a settlement with a large, dense population, organized around a complex of public structures.

PECTORAL—a decorative object worn on the chest.

PESTLE—a tapering staff used in conjunction with a mortar for pulverizing foodstuffs.

PETROGLYPH—a representation carved into stone.

PICTOGRAPH—a painted drawing on stone.

POCHTECA—professional traders of the Aztec culture.

POLISHED STONE—objects finished to a luster by rubbing with skin and a polishing powder.

PROJECTILE POINT—an object in the shape of a point, used as the head on a shaft which is hurled.

SCRAPER—a stone tool used in cleaning skins, smoothing wood.

SITE—a spatial unit which shows evidence of concentrated activity; *see* zone, territory.

SLASH-AND-BURN AGRICULTURE—a system of preparing forested land for cultivation, in which trees are cut and then burned in order to clear the area for planting.

SLIP—a thin mixture of clay and water applied to the surface of a ceramic vessel prior to firing to render it impermeable to water and to improve its color.

SPINDLE WHORL—a disk with a center hole for the spindle, used to manufacture thread.

SPOKESHAVE—a notched scraper used for shaping shafts.

STELA (*pl.*, STELAE)—carved stone monument.

SUPERPOSITION—the geological principle that any stratum is younger than those below it and older than those above it.

TERRITORY—a spatial unit consisting of several related zones.

ZONE—a spatial unit consisting of several related sites.

SELECTED BIBLIOGRAPHY

ACOSTA, JORGE. "Los últimos descubrimientos arquelógicos en Tula, Hgo. 1941," *Revista Mexicana de Estudios Antropológicos*, vol. 5 (1941), pp. 239–248.

ADAMS, ROBERT. *The Evolution of Urban Society*. Chicago: Aldine, 1966.

ARMILLAS, PEDRO. "The Arid Frontier of Mexican Civilization," *Transactions of the New York Academy of Science*, vol. 31, no. 6 (1969).

BERNAL, IGNACIO. *Mexico before Cortez: Art, History, and Legend*. New York: Doubleday, 1963.

COE, MICHAEL. *Mexico*. New York: Praeger, 1962.

————. *The Maya*. New York: Praeger, 1966.

COE, MICHAEL, AND FLANNERY, KENT. *Early Cultures and Human Ecology in South Coastal Guatemala*. Smithsonian Contributions to Anthropology, vol. 3, 1967.

CORTÉS, HERNÁNDO (HERNÁN). *The Despatches of Hernándo Cortés*. Trans. G. Folsom. New York: Wiley and Putnam, 1843.

DIAZ DEL CASTILLO, BERNAL. *The Discovery and Conquest of Mexico*. Trans. A. P. Maudsley. New York: Farrar, Straus and Cudahy, 1956.

DIEHL, RICHARD. Preliminary Report, University of Missouri Archaeological Project at Tula, Hidalgo, Mexico, 1970–1971 Field Seasons. Mimeographed. 1971.

FLANNERY, KENT. "The Olmec and the Valley of Oaxaca: A Model for Inter-Regional Interaction in Formative Times," in *Dumbarton Oaks Conference on the Olmec*, ed. E. P. Benson. Washington, D.C.: Dumbarton Oaks Research Library and Collection, 1968.

FURST, PETER. "The Olmec Were-Jaguar Motif in the Light of Ethnographic Reality," in *Dumbarton Oaks Conference on*

143

the Olmec, ed. E. P. Benson. Washington, D.C.: Dumbarton Oaks Research Library and Collection, 1968.

GAMIO, MANUEL. The Population of the Valley of Teotihuacán. Mexico, D.F.: Secretaría de Agricultura y Fomenta, 1922.

JIMÉNEZ MORENO, WIGBERTO. "Tula y los Toltecas según las fuentes historicas," Revista Mexicana de Estudios Antropológicos, vol. 5 (1941).

KATZ, FRIEDRICH. The Ancient American Civilizations. New York: Praeger, 1972.

KIRCHHOFF, PAUL. "Mesoamerica: Its Geographic Limits, Ethnic Composition and Cultural Characteristics," in Heritage of Conquest, ed. Sol Tax. New York: Macmillan, 1952.

KNOROZOV, Y. V. "The Problem of the Study of Maya Hieroglyphic Writing," American Antiquity, vol. 23 (1958), pp. 284–291.

MACNEISH, RICHARD. "A Summary of Subsistence," in Prehistory of the Tehuacán Valley, ed. D. S. Byers. Austin, Tex.: University of Texas Press, 1967.

MILLON, RENÉ. "Teotihuacan: Completion of Map of Giant Ancient City in the Valley of Mexico," Science, vol. 170, no. 3962 (1970), pp. 1077–1081.

PADDOCK, JOHN, ed. Ancient Oaxaca. Stanford, Calif.: Stanford University Press, 1966.

PARSONS, JEFFREY. "Prehistoric Settlement Patterns in the Texcoco Region, Mexico," Memoir no. 3, Museum of Anthropology, University of Michigan, 1971.

———. "Teotihuacán, Mexico and its Impact on Regional Demography," Science, vol. 162, no. 3856 (1968), pp. 872–877.

PROSKOURIAKOFF, TATIANA. "Historical Implications of a Pattern of Dates at Piedras Negras, Guatemala," American Antiquity, vol. 25 (1960), pp. 454–475.

RUZ, ALBERTO. The Civilization of the Ancient Maya. Mexico, D.F.: Instituto Nacional de Antropología e Historia, 1970.

SANDERS, WILLIAM. "The Central Mexican Symbiotic Region," in Prehistoric Settlement Patterns in the New World, ed. Gordon Willey. New York: Wenner-Gren Foundation for Anthropological Research, 1956.

———. The Cultural Ecology of the Teotihuacan Valley. Monograph. Department of Sociology and Anthropology, Pennsylvania State University, 1965.

SANDERS, WILLIAM, AND PRICE, BARBARA. *Mesoamerica: The Evolution of a Civilization*. New York: Random House, 1968.

SPINDEN, HERBERT. *Ancient Civilizations of Mexico and Central America*. New York: American Museum of Natural History, 1928.

THOMPSON, J. E. S. *Maya Hieroglyphic Writing*. Norman, Okla.: University of Oklahoma Press, 1971.

TOLSTOY, PAUL, AND PARADIS, LOUISE. "Early and Middle Preclassic Culture in the Basin of Mexico," *Science*, vol. 167, no. 3917 (1970), pp. 344–351.

VAILLANT, GEORGE C. *Early Cultures of the Valley of Mexico*. Anthropological Papers of the American Museum of Natural History, vol. 35, part 3, 1935.

WAUCHOPE, ROBERT, gen. ed. *Handbook of Middle American Indians*, vols. 1–11. Austin, Tex.: University of Texas Press, 1964–1971.

WEAVER, MURIEL PORTER. *The Aztecs, Maya and Their Predecessors*. New York: Seminar Press, 1972.

WILLEY, GORDON. *An Introduction to American Archaeology*, vol. 1. Englewood Cliffs, N.J.: Prentice-Hall, 1966.

WOLF, ERIC. *Sons of the Shaking Earth*. Chicago: University of Chicago Press, 1959.

INDEX

INDEX

INDEX

National Museum of Anthropology, Mexico City, 99
Nicaragua, 13, 111
nobility, Aztec, 127, 128
Noguera, Eduardo, 11
numeration, Mesoamerican, 16, 81, 84
Nuttall, Zelia, 9

Oaxaca, Valley of, 61, 64, 70, 73, 101, 116
obsidian, 13, 34
occupational specialization, 21, 22, 59, 65, 66, 105, 126–129
Olmec
  culture, 50, 52, 57, 59
  economic configuration, 62, 103, 111, 132
  influences, 59–60, 78
  region, 55, 56
  See also La Venta; San Lorenzo
Olmeca-Xicalanca people, 118

Palenque (Chiapas), 87, 91
Paleo-American period, 17, 41–43
Paleo-Indian period, *see* Paleo-American period
Parsons, Jeffrey, 68–69, 129
percussion flaking, 34, 38
Peru, 3, 11
Petén (Guatamala), 77
Piedras Negras (Guatamala), 87, 90
plant cultivation, 13, 17–18, 48, 67, 77, 105
pochteca (merchant-spies), 127, 128, 131
political relations, 21–22, 48, 68, 75, 97, 112–113, 129, 131; *see also* government

population, 21, 67, 75, 89, 105, 126, 129
Postclassic period, 17
pottery, 9, 10, 12; *see also* ceramics; figurines
pre-Mayan findings, 77–78
pressure chipping, 35
projectile points, 42, 43, 46
Proskouriakoff, Tatiana, 84, 90
Puebla, 60, 118, 120
Puuc style (Mayan), 99, 100
pyramids, 3, 57, 65, 70, 72, 74, 77, 78, 87, 107, 109

Q-complex, 11, 13
Quetzalcoatl (Toltec deity), 113
Quintana Roo, 75

regional interdependence, 21, 61–62, 101–103, 110–111, 129
religion, 21, 81, 84
ritual numbers, 13, 16
roof crests, 80
rural population, 21–22, 77–78, 128–129
Ruz, Alberto, 93

Sanders, William, 62, 64, 126, 129
San Lorenzo (Vera Cruz), 56–59
Santa Isabel Iztapan (State of Mexico), 42
Schroeder site (Durango), 111
sculpture, stone, 38, 52, 57, 59, 78, 80, 81, 89, 90, 107–110
Seler, Eduard, 6
semi-nomadic peoples, 119
settlement patterns
  contrasting types of, 74–75
  of Lowland Maya, 74–75, 78, 87, 89
  of Mitla, 117

INDEX

ABOUT THE AUTHOR AND THE PHOTOGRAPHER

SHIRLEY GORENSTEIN is associate professor of anthropology at Columbia University, New York City. She has directed archaeological expeditions to Mexico since 1964, and her writings include articles for *Natural History, American Antiquity,* and *American Anthropologist,* as well as a textbook, *Introduction to Archaeology.*

LEE BOLTIN is well known for his superb photographs of natural-history subjects. His photographs have appeared in *Natural History, Smithsonian, Scientific American,* and *American Heritage,* as well as in such books as *Art Before Columbus* and *Treasures of Ancient America.*